# Managing Scientists

# Managing Scientists
## *Leadership Strategies in Research and Development*

*Alice M. Sapienza*

WILEY-LISS

A JOHN WILEY & SONS, INC., PUBLICATION
New York • Chichester • Brisbane • Toronto • Singapore

**Address All Inquiries to the Publisher**
**Wiley-Liss, Inc., 605 Third Avenue, New York, NY 10158-0012**

**Copyright © 1995 Wiley-Liss, Inc.**

**Printed in the United States of America**

Sapienza, Alice M.
   Managing scientists : leadership strategies in research
and development / Alice M. Sapienza
      p.  cm.
   Includes index.
   ISBN 0-471-04367-2
   1. Research—Management.   2. Scientists—Relations.
3. Organizational behavior.   4. Management.   I. Title.
Q180.55.M3S27   1995
658.5'7—dc20                                        94-46618

The text of this book is printed on acid-free paper.

# FOREWORD
## Managing, Leading, and Managing *Well*

I believe that a good manager must also be a good leader. When I use the word *managing* throughout this book I mean two types of activities: 1) leading scientists as individuals, and 2) administering the research and development (R&D) organization. By the word *leading* I mean being an exemplar and inspiration to these scientists, as well as directing them in a course of action, in decision-making, and in problem solving. My emphasis throughout the book is on the activity of leading.

I wrote this book because I believe that managing scientists *well*, which I define as being a leader who is capable of achieving and maintaining an enthusiastic, energetic, and creative group of scientists (as well as administering the R&D organization effectively), is a very difficult task. Managing scientists entails leading people whose primary activity occurs between their ears. Moreover, the purpose of that activity is to generate knowledge and ideas, an endeavor that, in comparison with other organized activities, is oblique, hard to predict, unwieldy to measure, and difficult to judge except in hindsight. Because of these characteristics,

*v*

much of the conventional wisdom of administration, such as engineering-based planning and controlling, may not be directly applicable to research and development. (This often puts the manager of R&D at odds with those trained in traditional standards and metrics.)

Managing scientists is also difficult because scientific education and training produce groups of people who have conceptual frameworks, vocabularies, and discipline cultures that are very different from one another. And scientists are essentially trained to be solo contributors. (This does not rule out their directing a group of people engaged in their project, or collaborating with scientists on related projects.) That is why multidisciplinary teamwork and cross-functional communication and collaboration are not easily achieved within the R&D organization. Plus, scientists have moods, biases, quirks, and warts like the rest of us.

I contend that it is this combination of science (an oblique and unpredictable activity) and scientists (highly differentiated solo contributors who are also human beings) that is notoriously difficult to manage well. Achieving the right balance in R&D between, first, the ambiguity and challenge necessary to foster creativity and, second, the constraints necessary for producing results within time, cost, and perhaps commercial objectives is fraught with problems. Few scientists are able to strike that balance without making painful mistakes. For those of you who hope to be, who have chosen to be, or have discovered yourselves to be in the position of managing scientists, my objective is to help you avoid as many painful mistakes as possible.

## FOCUS OF THIS BOOK

I assume that you are trained as a scientist, that you have experienced or observed some of the difficulties facing managers of scientists, and that you appreciate the human side of research and development, whether you work in a university or a corporation, in a private foundation or a government laboratory.

My focus in this book is on improving the quality of the human interaction in the research and development organization. Although the principal activity is cognitive, the quality of the human interaction in R&D influences how creative the science and technology will be. There are important links between cognitive theory and behavioral theory that have inspired this book.

Let me be clear, however, that this is not meant to be an academic text, providing an overview of relevant cognitive and behavioral theories (although I include suggestions for interested readers). I have chosen to discuss only a limited number of topics—those I have come to appreciate as most important for managers of R&D to "get right."

I have also been quite selective in drawing only on theories that fulfill three personal criteria. First, they must be *robust*. There must be strong empirical evidence over time that the particular theory is valid and reliable. Second, they must be *parsimonious*. Some behavioral and cognitive theories I might have used are robust, but they are very cumbersome for managers to put into practice. Third, they must have *proved useful*, in my direct experience, to managers of research and development.

In the course of nearly a decade, I have experimented with a number of robust and parsimonious theories in my teaching of scientists and my consulting to R&D organizations, and I have discovered what works well. If you have an MBA as well as a PhD, or have taken courses in the social sciences, you will find, for example, that I emphasize David McClelland's theory of work-motivation needs, Fred Fiedler's theory of leadership style, Edgar Schein's model of culture, and so on. My reason is that their theories fulfill the above selection criteria. Other theories or models you may come across can be useful and I urge you to read more widely than this book. But this book is intentionally focused and selective.

Finally, I have tried hard to distill the knowledge I gained from my doctorate in organizational behavior, my general management experience, and my decade of teaching and consulting, so that my ideas can be simply put and readily applied (following the advice of a scientist who said to me: "Any fool can have a difficult idea!"). I begin the book, and your journey towards managerial wisdom, with what one scientist termed "eye-opening personal exercises." All chapters have been written for you to read, reflect upon, and read again. With each reading I hope you will bring different experiences to bear, drawing additional and deeper insights that you can apply directly to your own situation. If you approach the material with a willingness to learn in this way—that is, to read, reflect, and reread—I can state with confidence that:

1. You will learn something about yourself: what motivates you in the workplace and what is your preferred leadership (i.e., decision-making, problem-solving) style. I believe firmly that the beginning of wisdom and effectiveness in leadership comes from a better understanding of oneself and one's own strengths and weaknesses. From this comes heightened sensitivity to, and appreciation for, what motivates others and, in turn, an understanding of what is important in recruiting and training people. Such insights will be helpful as you think about your own career development and that of other scientists.

2. You will learn how to analyze the culture of your organization, with a view to discerning how that culture encourages or discourages creativity. Any organization more than a few months old will have a distinctive culture. Aspects of that culture will either foster the type of organiza-

tion you want to lead—with energetic, innovative, productive people—or discourage its development. You will learn what culture consists of, how it evolves, and how it can affect thinking and behaving. With this understanding you can assess the impact of culture on your own organization's performance and begin to change aspects of the culture that are detrimental to creativity.

3. You will learn how structure, size, and formal systems can be designed to improve the innovativeness of R&D. There is ample evidence that a manager who can develop an *organic* organization, characterized by (among other attributes) lateral relationships among scientists, can improve the creativity of R&D.

4. You will learn techniques for communicating and confronting effectively. Developing skills to deal with intragroup dynamics will help you develop collaboration when it is required; for example, in program and project teams. Simply putting qualified and capable scientists together on a task does not create a team. But understanding motivation, leadership style, communication, and confrontation will help you to promote teamwork among individuals as well as collaboration among larger groups, such as between chemistry and pharmacology, or between R&D and marketing.

5. Finally, because all organizations are imperfect, you will learn how to design and manage change in order to achieve an energetic, innovative, and productive organization. You will learn two fundamental types of change tactics, when and how to employ them, and what problems are likely to arise.

When you finish this book, my hope is that you will understand yourself and your colleagues better as people, that you will be able to analyze the R&D organization in a more systematic and rigorous manner, and that you will be better prepared to implement effective responses to the problems you have identified.

## POSTSCRIPT

Writing this book was provoked by my observing, when I teach and consult, that many scientists appear to be unaware that the human side of science is as legitimate a subject for learning as the phenomena of their own disciplines. Repeatedly, I watch managers fall into two traps. Either they act as if there is an algorithm for managing scientists, and if they expand the number of scientists and resources they will automatically increase by the same factor the number of future innovations their organization will produce. Or, they act as if innovation is completely stochastic, so that the goodness or badness of the social context is moot.

Both traps block learning. Learning to be an effective leader of R&D requires understanding your own and others' personal (as opposed to professional or technical) strengths and weaknesses, understanding the dynamics of human behavior, thoughtful analyses of the organizational conditions associated with success or failure, and seeking feedback regularly from those affected by your decisions.

Managing scientists well is an important and difficult task, as you have undoubtedly discovered from experience or observation. You have recognized that your training may not have prepared you for the task. I hope this book will help.

# ACKNOWLEDGMENTS

Books have long lead times and many influences. I could, justifiably, go back to my own studies in chemistry at Stonehill College and acknowledge my professors for effectively starting the journey that is bearing this fruit (I do hereby acknowledge them). More recent influences must include Paul Lawrence, professor of organizational behavior in my masters's and doctoral work at Harvard Business School, and Bill Curran, who invited me to develop a course in organizational behavior for his executive program at Harvard School of Public Health. Through Bill, I met the memorable scientists who really inspired me to write this book: the students in those programs who patiently helped me to understand their unique issues, and the scientist–managers who shared their stories with me and provided the case material I use in the executive program. To Bill and all these people, my deepest gratitude. The book also required the "jump start" provided by Mike Williams and his contacts with John Wiley. Thanks, Mike, for the prod. . . . In the heat of the writing effort, I benefited enormously from the help of Diana Stork, Desmond Fitzgerald, and Dianne Mahany. Towards the end of the effort, Joe Lombardino provided much important feedback on project management and organizational change. During the entire effort, Ivan Jensen cheerfully slogged through the work with me, line by line. Many, many thanks. . . . I also received encouragement and assistance from Susan King of John Wiley (with whom I shared many cups of coffee in New York City) and her colleagues. My appreciation to them for making the hope a reality.

# CONTENTS

*xiii*

# Contents

# Managing Scientists

CHAPTER ONE

# INTRODUCTION
## The Larger Context of Scientific R&D

The eight chapters that follow address what might be termed the "inner workings" of the research and development (R&D) organization. This chapter briefly reviews both the larger political–economic and institutional–strategic contexts of R&D, to clarify the sources of some of the external pressures on you as manager. The remainder of the book requires that you differentiate problems arising from these external pressures (which are unlikely to be problems in the quality of the human interaction) from those arising within the R&D organization itself (which are likely to be such problems).

## THE POLITICAL–ECONOMIC CONTEXT

The political economy of scientific R&D in all the industrialized nations can be illustrated by the following statement from the report of the U.S. National Critical Technologies Panel to then-President Bush:

We most recently have been reminded . . . of the crucial role that technology plays in military competitiveness. It is equally clear that technology plays a similar role in the economic competitiveness of nations.

. . . In an environment of intensifying global competition, deployment of technology is becoming the strategic battlefield of the international marketplace.[1]

Although it seems obvious today, the link between scientific and technological progress on the one hand and economic competitiveness on the other was made comparatively recently. The argument was put forth in the early 1900s by a Dutch economist, van Gelderen, and elaborated by the Russian economist, Kondratiev, whose name has become synonymous with "long waves" or long cycles of economic growth. (Kondratiev's 1926 paper was entitled: "The Long Waves in Economic Life."[2])

According to one framework, we are in the fifth Kondratiev or long cycle of economic growth since the Industrial Revolution.[3] The first long cycle was stimulated by scientific and technological advances in, especially, textile production; the second by advances that produced the steam engine and railroads; the third by advances in electrical machinery and heavy engineering; and the fourth by advances in mass production.

The fifth Kondratiev cycle, which began around 1980, was catalyzed by earlier semiconductor and microelectronics discoveries that revolutionized computing. These discoveries, and others like biotechnology and new materials, are deemed to be of strategic importance because they are expected to transform world economies of the twenty-first century in much the same way as steam and electricity transformed the world at the turn of the twentieth century. According to one report by the U.S. Office of Technology Assessment:

2

These inventions [steam and electricity] did much more than improve on the way things had been done in the past. They changed basic conceptions about the limits of human ingenuity, removing seemingly insurmountable barriers. Moreover, they had effects going far beyond the market for which specific inventions were originally developed. Each cluster of technologies led to rapid growth in wealth, standards of living, and employment.[4]

The current long wave, catalyzed by the new emerging technologies, is different from past times of economic growth, however. During prior Kondratiev cycles, most of the scientific and technological advances occurred primarily by increments, the result in part of what de Solla Price called "scholarly bricklaying."[5] But in the post-World War II period a number of radical discoveries, such as very large scale integration computing technology, genetic engineering, and superconductivity, have triggered rapidly advancing science frontiers. Insights gained about one problem illuminate questions that may have been asked earlier but remained unanswered, or only partially answered. Knowledge "cascades" quickly throughout numerous fields of science and new technologies emerge, some of which catalyze other radical discoveries. As a consequence, you will be under intense pressure simply to keep abreast of the increasingly rapid pace of advance of the science and technology relevant to your organization.

You will also be under pressure from government policy and legislation. During the past two decades, the response of governments in all the industrialized nations to the perceived strategic importance of science and technology has been similar. They have identified public-sector R&D likely to be the source of radical discoveries, in order to ensure its support. And they have designed incentives for private-sector investment in and development of potential innovations, especially by means of alliances between public-sector and commercial organizations. Such policy and legislation reflect governments' concern with science and technology and its economic impact, but their effect is to put pressure on you to "deliver," and quickly.

The political–economic context of R&D is not the only source of pressure on you as manager. The institutional strategic context also exerts pressure by and through, especially, resource allocation. The next section describes some of the strategic and portfolio processes driving R&D decisions in all scientific and technical organizations.

## THE INSTITUTIONAL STRATEGIC CONTEXT

The word *strategy* originally referred to the overall plan for deploying people and equipment in battle so as to overcome the enemy. As the earlier reference to "the strategic battle-field" of economic competitiveness suggests, the word has now come to refer to the general blueprint by which institutions seek to grow, flourish, and do better than their competitors. Because every institution has competitors—for political power, for customers, for legitimacy, for funding—"strategy" is applicable to nations and to universities, as well as to corporations.

The process by which strategy emerges, *strategic planning*, can be described by one of three levels of managerial sophistication. At the lowest level managers *opportunistically react* to events, trends, and issues that attract their attention. For example, managers of a high-technology corporation could decide to enter a number of strategic alliances with startups, primarily because of tax and other incentives provided by government policy and legislation. However, without an explicit management decision and effort to move beyond this level of sophistication, minimalist strategy and performance are the likely consequences of opportunistic and reactive "strategic planning."

At a higher level of sophistication, managers attempt to *position* their institution according to the familiar SWOT paradigm: assessing the Strengths and Weaknesses of the institution and the Opportunities and Threats in the environment. For example, managers of the same high-technology corporation could decide to enter government-encouraged strategic alliances (Opportunity) only with those startups that filled an identified gap in their R&D capability (Weakness). Positioning strategy can result in satisfactory, albeit not outstanding, strategy and performance.

At the highest level of sophistication, managers attempt to be *instrumental* in shaping the environment. Instrumental strategic planning does not take the environment as a given; rather, managers attempt to envision what might be and then plan and actively work to achieve that. For example, managers of this high-technology corporation could decide that the next radical discovery in superconductivity is likely to emerge from work underway at a relatively obscure university. They would fund that research and set up intense linkages between corporate and university scientists, so that the corporation might achieve first-mover advantages from any possible breakthrough.

In the abstract, instrumental strategic planning involves four steps:

- Defining the strategic vision for the institution.
- Assessing the environment (both competitive position and the turbulence of external forces, including rapidly advancing science frontiers).

- Determining institutional goals and tactics, given the strategic vision and assessment of the environment and internal capabilities.
- Experimenting, ensuring feedback on the action, evaluating performance, etc.

The purpose of first crafting a vision and sharing it widely within the institution is to focus people's efforts and inspire them over the long term. This is the only step that can be accomplished, in the sense of completing and setting aside, because *strategy* must define a trajectory for the institution over at least a decade. The three remaining steps essentially set and reset the coordinates of that trajectory and ensure the momentum necessary for the institution to achieve the ideal described by the strategic vision.

As you might imagine, an enormous analytic effort is involved—to determine competitive position (e.g., with regard to current rivals, potential entrants, suppliers, buyers, and providers of substitutes[6]); to identify the most turbulent external forces; and to evaluate institutional capability. The outcome of this process is the strategy that is intended to be the framework and guide for the subsequent resource allocation decisions by which the strategy will be implemented.

The reality of strategy implementation and associated portfolio decisions in R&D, however, is fraught with problems that will put additional pressure on you as manager. Strategy ceases to be abstract when it must be implemented, because no resource (money, space, time, staff, equipment) exists in a vacuum. Every resource comes with people, vested interests, and actual or perceived power attached.

For example, one midsize European company specializing in ceramics and composite materials decided in 1989 that by the year 2000 they would be a world leader in a number of new materials areas. To achieve this vision, top management realized they had to shift overall R&D resources from one division with a stable market share but maturing ceramics technology to another division with small market share but potentially enormous growth from developments in new materials. The manager of new materials R&D soon realized (not surprisingly) that the ceramics manager strongly opposed the shift in resources and attempted to discredit the capabilities of the new-materials scientists. In addition to being under pressure from rapidly advancing frontiers in new-materials science, this manager also found himself under pressure to defend the company's strategic shift in resources.

Portfolio decisions focus on projects within the R&D organization and take place (ideally) within the context of the institution's strategic plan. Given constraints on money, all organizations must determine which projects take high priority for continuation. On an annual or other regular basis, managers of R&D must examine the scientific and technical feasibility of current projects, their progress to date, what progress other institutions have made (and, thus, the likely competitive scenario), and the expected outcome from the completed project, whether that outcome be product sales or enhanced positioning for outside funding. Needless to say, each project has people, vested interests, and power attached. You will be under pressure from the debates about project-ranking criteria, key assumptions, reliability of information, accuracy of data, organizational capabilities, and so on.

Ideally, institutional strategy and portfolio implementation processes should produce rational R&D resource allocation decisions. As manager of R&D, however, you will discover (or have discovered already) that the reality can be quite different. Power, politics, and having the "ear" of the "right" person might be as close to rational processes as the institution is able to come.

The following chapters, reviewed below, make the heroic

assumption that all people in both R&D and the larger institution agree with the strategic and portfolio decisions made by management. Your task is only to achieve and maintain an enthusiastic, energetic, and creative group of scientists, and to administer the R&D organization effectively.

## REVIEW OF FOLLOWING CHAPTERS

Chapters 2 and 3 are intended to be read next. Each contains an important exercise (the "eye-opening personal exercises" noted in the Foreword) whose validity requires that you complete the exercise in the order in which it appears in the text. Results from these exercises are referred to throughout the book.

Chapter 2 begins with the central topic of motivation and contains the first exercise, which will provide insight into your own work-motivation needs. An illustration of three scientific careers is then used to demonstrate how to interpret what others say and do, with a view to understanding better their work-motivation needs. The chapter concludes with a discussion of some of the implications for your career development as well as for recruiting, training, and promoting your staff.

Your ordering of work motivation needs is related to your preferred leadership style. Chapter 3, which contains the second exercise, emphasizes that leadership style should fit certain elements of the work situation. An illustration of two managers of research, each of whom exemplifies a particular style, is provided to assist you in interpreting your own leadership style and the styles of people in your organization. The chapter concludes with a discussion of some of the implications of leadership style for you, your boss, and your staff.

Chapter 4 describes a model of organizational culture and illustrates how the three "levels" of culture can be discerned in your organization. Using several examples, the chapter explores how this culture, as reflected in the core beliefs of the larger social context, can either foster an energetic, productive, innovative R&D organization or prohibit it from developing.

In addition to organizational culture, other aspects of the larger social context are important in fostering innovation. Chapter 5 begins with an overview of creativity and then examines the potential impact of organization structure, size, and formal systems on the creativity of R&D as a whole.

Chapter 6 tackles one of the most important tasks of the leader: communicating effectively. This chapter discusses, first, the complex process of communication, providing ample illustrations of the many problems that can occur in simple written and oral communication within the R&D organization. Illustrations of solutions are also provided. Next, the chapter explores the message that is communicated, intentionally or unintentionally, using an illustration of three scientists talking about a merger. The chapter concludes by describing recent communications research that suggests that the type of medium used to transmit your message should be matched to key attributes of that message.

Chapter 7 focuses on the likely sources of conflict in R&D and on confrontation as the most effective means of dealing with conflict. Confrontation of differences is critical to ensuring the appropriate environment of intellectual challenge of ideas in the R&D organization.

In Chapter 8, motivation and leadership style are linked to intragroup dynamics, focusing on collaboration within program and project teams. The ideal team composition according to work motivation needs of the members is described. Then, project life-cycle theory is presented in terms of group behavior and how the style of the project leader must change according to life-cycle stage. The chapter concludes with a discussion of the matrix organization.

Because no organization is perfect, Chapter 9 addresses the management of change. In this chapter, two fundamental models of organizational change, and how and when each should be employed, are described. The language of the manager, especially the imagery employed, is emphasized as an important tool in the management of change. Again, illustrations of practical change techniques are provided.

When you have finished reading the book, you should understand yourself and your colleagues better as people, you should be able to analyze the R&D organization in a more systematic and rigorous manner, and you should be better prepared to implement effective responses to the problems you have identified. In short, you should be better able to manage *well*.

## NOTES

1. Report of the National Critical Technologies Panel, Arlington, VA, March 1991, pp. i, 1.
2. The link between science and technology and economic growth is discussed by Peter Dicken in *Global Shift*, New York: Harper & Row, 1986.
3. This framework is presented in Christopher Freeman and Carlotta Perez, "Structural Crises of Adjustment, Business Cycles, and Investment Behaviour," in Dosi, et al., *Technical Change and Economic Theory*, London: Pinter, 1988.
4. U.S. Office of Technology Assessment, Technology and the American Economic Transition, Washington, D.C., 1988, p. 15.
5. Derek de Solla Price, *Little Science, Big Science . . . and Beyond*, New York: Columbia University Press, 1986, p. 58.
6. See, for example, Michael Porter, *Competitive Strategy*, New York: The Free Press, 1990.

# UNDERSTANDING WHAT MOTIVATES YOU AND WHAT MOTIVATES OTHERS

Imagine this. You wake up before the alarm goes off, with a feeling of joyful anticipation about the day ahead. Taking your coffee with you in the car, you arrive at the laboratory before most of your coworkers. At some point in the early afternoon, you and your colleagues go to the cafeteria for a sandwich, continuing an intense discussion about the experiment that is being planned. Back at your desk, the time goes by so quickly that when someone asks when you're leaving, you notice with regret that it is already 6:20 PM.

## WHAT IS MOTIVATION?

The word "motivation" comes from the Latin *movere*, meaning "to move"—not in the sense of picking up a beaker and moving it to the sink, but in the sense of being moved to action. When the term "motivated" is used in this book, it means that people are moved to the enthusiastic and energetic action illustrated by the above scenario. When people are "motivated," there is little they cannot accomplish.

Resource constraints? They will find other means. Seemingly intractable problem? They will keep turning the problem on its head and persist until they find a solution.

Being "motivated" implies that you love your job, literally. Certainly, some days will be closer to the ideal than others. But in a "motivated" R&D organization, you, your colleagues, your boss, and your subordinates should feel pleasurable anticipation about work, and the time at work should pass quickly and with joy.

How do you create a research and development organization in which most of the people are motivated most of the time?

To begin, management research provides ample support for the following recommendations.[1]

First, working conditions must be reasonable. Safety in the laboratory must be ensured; space must be at least adequate and decently appointed; the required equipment must be available to do the job, and so forth.

Second, you must have competent people trained appropriately for their job.

Third, people must believe that their effort will lead to job performance (e.g., discovering the genetic component of a disease); they must believe that this performance will lead to certain outcomes (e.g., project success and personal recognition by their scientific peers); and they must value the outcomes.

Fourth, people must be treated and paid fairly in your organization, as compared with similar organizations.

Lastly, people should not be asked to perform the impossible, but they should be challenged to go beyond what they initially see as their limits.

It should be obvious that people will *not* be motivated if:

- The conditions under which they work are hazardous or fundamentally problematic.

- They are not competent or not trained properly for the job.
- They do not believe their effort will lead to performance, that performance will lead to an outcome, or they do not value the outcome.
- Their treatment (including pay and benefits) is not fair.
- They are not challenged to excel.

These are common-sense propositions, and the discussion in this chapter assumes that they are not an issue in your organization. But in addition to these basic conditions, research indicates that a motivated R&D organization also requires a fit among 1) personal competencies, 2) job demands, and 3) organizational characteristics.[2]

The three spheres in the Venn diagram (page 14) illustrating this fit have been further subdivided into technical and human aspects. *Personal competencies* include education, training, and skills (technical aspects), and confidence, willingness to take risks, tolerance of ambiguity, work-related needs, and leadership style (human aspects). *Job demands* include those usually listed in the job description, such as responsibilities, knowledge, required skills, and experience (technical aspects), and others usually not listed, such as patience, diplomacy, good listening skills, and sense of humor (human aspects). *Organizational characteristics* include size, structure, and formal systems of the R&D organization (technical aspects), and the culture of that organization (the human aspect).

When the basic conditions described earlier are met and there is a good fit among these three spheres of influence, the R&D organization will exhibit an almost audible "hum" that is the hallmark of people working enthusiastically and energetically, loving their jobs.

The reason for emphasizing the fit between the human

## Motivation: The Required Fit

### Personal Competencies

*Technical Aspects*—Education, skills, training, etc.
*Human Aspects*—Work-motivation needs, leadership style, etc.

### Job Demands

*Technical Aspects*—Responsibilities, experience, etc.
*Human Aspects*—Patience, diplomacy, good listener, etc.

### Organizational Characteristics

*Technical Aspects*—Structure, systems, etc.
*Human Aspects*—Culture, etc.

aspects of personal competencies and job demands in this and the following chapters is that most of us are adept at matching the technical aspects of personal competencies and job demands. (Organizational characteristics are discussed in Chapters 4 and 5.) Job descriptions and systematic organizational processes match people to jobs on the basis of education, training, skills, and experience. But we are generally less adept at ensuring a fit between the human aspects of the job and of the person.

Consider the job of R&D director. If you were to write a description of some of the required human aspects of this job you might include:

Required: Must be able to "take the heat" and buffer the external forces on the organization when necessary; to shield scientists from inappropriate organizational demands while handling these demands diplomatically; to make the tough decisions and stick to them; to be content with working behind the scenes in successful times and to be willing to take the blame upfront in problem times. . . .

Or the job of project manager:

Required: Must be able to balance the apparently irreconcilable demands made by the functional managers involved in the project; to deal with difficult team members with grace and good humor; to develop the close collaboration required for efficient project handovers; to understand and deal effectively with the emotional termination of successful or unsuccessful projects. . . .

Or the job of lead scientist:

Required: Must be able to focus single-mindedly on the problem no matter what the distractions; to remain hopeful under conditions of failure; to inspire those working with you to persist; never to let the organization get you down. . . .

To help you match the human aspects of the job to those of the person, beginning with yourself, is the objective of this and the third chapter.

## UNDERSTANDING WHAT MOTIVATES YOU

Being an effective leader begins with a better understanding of oneself and one's own strengths and weaknesses. Much of this managerial wisdom comes with learning from mistakes made on the job, but a certain amount can be gained by reflective self-analysis, which is the purpose of the following exercise, below.

NOTICE: This exercise must be completed and scored *before* you read the explanation and discussion that follow. Ensure that you have an uninterrupted 30 minutes to complete the exercise.

### First Exercise in Managerial Wisdom

Work-Related Needs. There are a number of exercises by which you can gain insight into your personality. The one used in this chapter is based on a model proposed by David McClelland, a psychologist, who states that each individual has a unique ordering of three work-related needs.[3] Each of us has a need for **power**, which he defines as a need to influence a group of people to attain a desired outcome. Each of us has a need for **achievement**—a need to set an individual goal and work until we reach it. And each of us has a need for **affiliation**—a need to develop and maintain good interpersonal relations with our coworkers.

Before you read further, take a piece of paper and portray *graphically* (using whatever image comes to mind) what you believe is your own unique ordering of these needs. Save this illustration.

There are three pictures that follow. For *each* picture:[4]

- Look at the picture for about one minute.
- Cover the picture and, in 10 minutes, write a story about the picture that is continuous, dramatic, and interesting. Don't try to answer all the questions that were next to the picture but use them to help you weave the story. Use separate sheets of paper for the stories.
- Be imaginative. There are no right or wrong stories.

## Runners and Picnic

Who are the people?
What are their names?
What are their roles in life?
What are their relationships to each other?
What has led up to this situation?
What is happening right now?
What is each person thinking, saying, trying to do?
What does each person want from whom?
What will happen to each person in the future?
How will it all end?

## The Airplane

Who are the people?
What are their names?
What are their roles in life?
What are their relationships to each other?
What has led up to this situation?
What is happening right now?
What is each person thinking, saying, trying to do?
What does each person want from whom?
What will happen to each person in the future?
How will it all end?

## The Office

Who are the people?
What are their names?
What are their roles in life?
What are their relationships to each other?
What has led up to this situation?
What is happening right now?
What is each person thinking, saying, trying to do?
What does each person want from whom?
What will happen to each person in the future?
How will it all end?

## Interpreting the Thematic Apperception Tests

The pictures on pages 18–20 constitute a portion of the thematic apperception tests (TAT) that McClelland and colleagues use to determine work-related needs. The theme is work, although that may not have been apparent to you (sets of pictures are available for many other themes). "Apperception" means that you interpret the pictures in light of your own experience. "Test" is simply a psychologic instrument for measuring, in this case, your unique ordering of work-related needs.

To interpret the thematic apperception test, first read through each story and decide if it shows the following.

**Power.** One or more characters in the story are concerned with attaining or maintaining control of the means for influencing others (e.g., organizational position). Influencing others can include inspiring or convincing others. The relationship of people in the story is usually of superior to subordinate.

**Achievement.** One or more characters in the story are concerned with their own personal success in competition with some standard of excellence (external or self-imposed). The success represents a unique attainment for the character(s), and there may be references to long-term effort by the character(s) to achieve this success.

**Affiliation.** One or more characters in the story are concerned with establishing, maintaining, or restoring positive (i.e., warm and companionate) interpersonal relationships. The story may also describe a social gathering, and/or it may utilize dialogue among the characters.

When you read the stories, underline key words and phrases and then transcribe them to another sheet of paper under the heading that best fits the work-related need (power, achievement, affiliation). Key words and phrases to look for include: *power* (titles, instrumental activity to influence or inspire, concern with organizational action or success, strategy); *achievement* (numbers, means–end statements, winning, doing as well as or better than another, concern with how well a task is being performed); *affiliation* (friends, statements describing emotions about relationships, helping, need for positive response from another).

Then, review the following examples (composites from actual stories completed by scientists) and think about which are most similar to your own.

## Runners and Picnic

**Power.** Hal has brought his family to the park on Sunday afternoon. His twin daughters, Kate and Emily, went off jogging with their brother, Lou. Aileen, Hal's wife, had set out the food and now they are talking about his plans for the company. Hal quit the corporation where he worked to start his own firm several years ago ("Gene-Chip"), and it's doing well. He hopes to be able to hire three more people and is describing to Aileen his strategy for collaborating with academic scientists, in the hope of getting in on the ground floor for the anticipated breakthrough in biosensor development. On Monday, Hal will meet with investors to discuss the possible acquisition of a small startup firm that will complement Gene-Chip's expertise.

**Achievement.** It's 12:15 PM and Joe has again taken his lunch hour to run 5 miles through a nearby park. He's hoping to compete in the Boston marathon in 2 weeks and needs all the practice he can get. Two women are out jogging as he runs by. Joe thinks they are accountants in his company, but he's not sure. He checks his watch and tries to sprint for about 5 minutes before concluding his run and returning to work.

**Affiliation.** Lois and Rob have been going out for some time, but the relationship is in difficulty. Rob has persuaded Lois to join him for a picnic in the hope of getting to the root of their problem. Two of their friends, Sheryl and Tamara, are jogging behind another runner and just waved to them as they went by, but Lois hardly noticed. Rob is upset, but he will try to talk it out with Lois and decide what they need to do. Unfortunately, the relationship does not last. Lois eventually marries another man, and Rob remains single.

# The Airplane

**Power.** Lee and Harry are getting off the last flight from New York City, where they spent the day meeting with analysts to discuss a discovery their company made recently in robotics design. Lee is VP of strategy and Harry is her new assistant, with an excellent background in statistics and economics. Lee is sure that Harry's graphs convinced the analysts that the stock price for their company will go up rapidly. She is looking forward to meeting with the president in the morning to tell him about their discussion and the expected improvement in the firm's market value.

**Achievement.** Laura has just returned from a tour of colleges with her father. She is tired, but she thinks she will choose the University of Wisconsin because of its physics program. Laura was impressed with the facilities there and had already begun to think about continuing an experiment she had run last summer while a student intern at MIT. If she is successful she will be eligible for a National Science Foundation award and scholarship. The stewardess says good night as they leave the plane.

**Affiliation.** The stewardess, Pat, smiles at the couple getting off the plane. She has watched during the flight as they got to know one another and then laughed together over the movie. While she was serving them drinks, she fantasized that he would call the woman tomorrow, they would be suited to each other, and they would get engaged very soon. When Pat gets home, she will go out to dinner with her family and another couple and tell them this story.

## The Office

**Power.** Maria, CEO of a large consumer products corporation, has just asked the vice president of planning to look at the report Jamal prepared. She will be meeting with the board tomorrow to discuss her strategic plan, and Jamal (seated) was asked to analyze the prior 5 years' sales in Asia. She is hoping that the data will convince the board that the company must expand that division. She has been meeting all day with her VPs, and will go back to them with Jamal's report for another lengthy strategy session.

**Achievement.** Dr. Dan Eliot is anxious about his upcoming meeting with the patent attorney, Mike Farrell, who is coming out of his office. Lia Murphy, the secretary, just told him Dan had arrived. Dan is a biochemist who has discovered a new process for targeting monoclonal antibodies in humans—a discovery that could almost guarantee funding for his post-docs for the next few years. Although he is pleased with the scientific accomplishment after nearly 6 years of work, Dan is realistic about the financial pressures on the university. If he can patent his process, he may be able to expand his laboratory and develop an internationally recognized "center of excellence.".

**Affiliation.** Leslie is delighted to see Paul and Greg talking collegially in her office after all the difficulties she had when Greg was first hired. He appeared to be very arrogant, and Paul often burst into her office threatening to quit. Leslie spent weeks counseling Paul, explaining that Greg was really unsure of the contribution he could make. Eventually, Leslie succeeded in helping Paul and Greg work collaboratively, and she noted that others now sought out Greg for lunch or coffee.

Consider what your own stories have in common with the sample stories. Note that each "power" story has an *organizational perspective* and describes strategy, planning, and the future. The protagonist—Hal, Lee, Maria—is concerned with what will happen to the organization. In contrast, each "achievement" story has an *individual perspective*, and that is an important clue to the difference between achievement and power needs. The protagonist—Joe, Laura, Dan—is concerned about his or her personal goal (marathon, college, experiment). Notice also, in the story about Joe, the numeric specificity (12:15 PM, 5 miles, 2 weeks, 5 minutes) that is often characteristic of a person with high achievement needs. Each "affiliation" story focused on the *relationships* among individuals—Lois and Rob, the couple on the plane, Paul and Greg. Notice that the story is more concerned with how people interact than with what they do.

One or more of your stories might contain elements of all three needs. In this case, try to judge in what proportion each appears. Or, it might be difficult to interpret any of the needs from one story. In that case, try to infer what the other stories reveal. What is important is that you gauge from the stories *taken as a whole* what your unique ordering of needs might be.

When you have read and reread your stories, written the key words and themes on a worksheet, and compared the stories with the examples, again portray graphically what they illustrate as your unique ordering of motivation needs. Compare this with what you initially deduced. Are the illustrations different? (They usually are.)

After you interpret the material, you might ask at least two people to read the stories and then reflect on your own and their interpretations. Getting an outside perspective is very useful.

## Some Implications of McClelland's Theory

Our ordering of work-related needs, in particular our dominant need, constitutes a major human aspect of our particular personal competencies. McClelland and his colleagues have found, from longitudinal studies of people on the job, that:[5]

- The ordering of needs is a stable part of personality. It does not change over time or with different types of work experience (i.e., one cannot "grow" one's need for power by moving into general management).

- Each person's ordering of needs is a very good predictor of long-term patterns of behavior, *not* necessarily of a single action.
- There are no consistent gender differences in work-related needs. Women do not have higher affiliation needs than men; men do not have higher achievement or power needs than women.
- People with a very high need for achievement are critical to the scientific and technologic progress of organizations. They do well as individual contributors but are generally not interested in managing others. People with a dominant need for achievement are primarily interested in how well *they* are doing, not how well the *organization* is doing.
- People with a very high need for power are associated with making dramatic organizational innovations and with bringing about radical change. They are likely to seek positions of leadership and to be impatient with positions that do not give them scope for influencing others. People with a dominant need for power coupled with a low need for affiliation may be able to make difficult organizational decisions without worrying about being liked or disliked because of their decisions.
- People with a very high need for affiliation perform best when the demands of their job enable them to satisfy their need for establishing and maintaining positive working relationships (e.g., middle and project management). However, they may be anxious about how well they are liked, and they may violate larger group norms (e.g., the division) in favor of the small group which they manage (e.g., a project team).

What do these research findings mean for you?

If you have a very high need for power, you are likely to enjoy general management and unlikely to be happy (motivated) in a job that does not provide you with opportunities to lead. If you have a very high need for affiliation, you are likely to enjoy middle and project management and unlikely to be happy (motivated) in a job in which you work essentially alone. If you have a very high need for achievement, you are likely to enjoy being lead scientist and working primarily as individual contributor and unlikely to be happy (motivated) in a job in which your primary task is managing others. These are just guidelines, because we have a combination of needs, but they are important guidelines that are referred to throughout this book.

Consider again the Venn diagram and the two top spheres of personal competencies and job demands. Assuming that the basic conditions listed earlier are met (e.g., safety, equity, goal challenge), your own motivation, loving your job, depends a good deal on the proper matching of the technical and human aspects of your job with your own technical competencies and work-related needs.

Are you in the right job? Perhaps you have been struggling with the job and wondering about your career. If the fit of the human aspects is not quite right, you may be able to restructure your job and improve the match. For example, if you have a high need for power and a low need for affiliation, you may want an assistant with a high need for affiliation, to focus on the human relationships within your organization. Or, you might ask to take on responsibilities beyond the job description that allow you scope to do what you love to do and do not detract from your current task. Or, you might begin a discussion with your boss to plan a career path that will put you in a position for which you are better suited. Or, you might change organizations or change jobs.

# UNDERSTANDING WHAT MOTIVATES OTHERS

Short of becoming an expert in administering and interpreting thematic apperception tests, what can you do to understand better what motivates other people, such as your boss, your colleagues, or your subordinates? You can observe their behavior, listen to them, and observe them over time. The insights you have gained from a better understanding of yourself will also help, as will the analysis of the following story of three scientists and the careers they chose.[6]

## Three Scientific Careers

In the early 1970s Shelly and Geoff, two PhD engineers from the University of Wisconsin, went to work in the R&D division of a large multinational corporation. Shelly came directly from a post-doc position and was immediately impressed with the corporate research facilities:

> The university laboratory in which I'd been running my experiments had only the "bare bones," so I was constantly scrounging equipment from other departments, or buying it myself. When I first went to work in the corporate R&D facility I thought: Here is everything I could possibly want. It was like a science fiction movie with all this fantastic equipment!

Her colleague, Geoff, recalled something quite different:

> I think there were about 200 people in R&D and we all got to know one another very quickly. I also recall that

there were no formal distribution lists for information—you got it over coffee in the morning, or at lunchtime when everyone sat together, managers as well as technicians. We all knew each other, from the most junior person to the most senior manager.

About 7 years after they started, the director of R&D who had hired Shelly and Geoff decided to move to a smaller, more entrepreneurial company. Shelly had made a major scientific discovery, resulting in a product expected to earn enormous profits. However, she was kept on a project looking for successors to that product and was becoming bored. The director was readily able to persuade both Shelly and Geoff to join him at the smaller company, where he had the opportunity to build a world-class technology capability.

At the new company, Shelly applied her earlier strategy and logic to another engineering problem, and Geoff worked in a related department. All went smoothly until about 3 years later, when the director accepted a position in Asia and chose Geoff to succeed him as manager. For Geoff, the result of that promotion was initially traumatic:

I don't mind admitting that this was one of the most difficult periods of my entire working career. Not only was I suddenly moved from a bench position to management but also the relationship Shelly and I had became very tense because of my promotion. Although we didn't talk about it, I could see that she was hurt and furious at being "passed over."

When I think about what my boss did, and I truly believe he made the right decision, I wonder if I could have done the same at that time. Shelly is undoubtedly a better development engineer than I. But I was the better choice for manager, because I soon discovered how much I enjoyed it and how well I accomplished it.

*30*

That is, I enjoyed it after Shelly and I began speaking to one another again.

I'm still not sure, if it had been up to me, that I would have been able to make this decision. Shelly and I both suffered. Although we eventually resolved our problems, it took three difficult months for us to sort it out.

It was obvious to Geoff that Shelly was on the verge of another breakthrough discovery, but their firm was struggling. Earnings had been flat, and there were no new products likely to be ready for several years. As a result, corporate management began to put pressure on Geoff to stop the project, but he demured.

Shelly was only partly aware of these company pressures:

Well, I knew something was going on when corporate management showed up in the laboratory. They didn't say anything; just walked around with Geoff in tow.

Geoff let us continue to work on the project. In fact, I don't remember any decisions one way or the other. The truth is, I just went on working. Perhaps Geoff or someone went to headquarters to support us, but I was happily unaware of this. As long as our salaries were being paid, as long as I had all the technicians I needed and the right equipment, I just kept on with the experiments.

In 1984, Shelly and her team delivered a paper that made it clear how important their achievement was in the field. Even though the actual product would not be on the market for several years, Shelly decided to leave the company and go back to a university:

Yes, I enjoyed the work at the two companies, but I left because, once I have solved the problems in principle,

I need to move on. I did not want to find myself type-cast as expert in only one particular field and being bored by having to find successor products.

When Geoff described his tenure as director, he was quite honest about the conflicting emotions he felt:

During this period I had terrible indigestion, all the time, from stress. When Shelly left for the university I was very upset to lose our most creative engineer. But she said to me: "Look on the bright side. You'll feel so much better when I leave." She was right. But of course I would work with Shelly tomorrow, even if it meant a return of that stress and gastric misery.

I discovered as a new manager that my staff of engineers could be divided into two groups. When I heard that anyone from the first group had an appointment with me I would look forward to a nice, friendly discussion. But I also discovered that, when they walked out of my office, I was usually no wiser than before they came in.

The second group of engineers was very small in number, for which I was grateful. Because when I heard *they* had an appointment, I would fantasize about disappearing before they came in, because I knew they were going to be blunt—quite outspoken about what I had or had not done—and they were going to be demanding. But I soon learned that when they left my office I was definitely a wiser manager. They were the people I and the company needed, even if I did not want to admit it then, and Shelly most certainly fell into that category.

Towards the end of 1984 Geoff hired Ichiro Naiti, a

PhD working in a government defense laboratory, as replacement for Shelly. When Ichiro described his impressions of the company, the attraction was clear:

For the first time in my experience I saw an organization in which engineering and manufacturing worked together, really collaborated. And they had come up with a tremendous breakthrough.

I was brought in initially as Shelly's replacement, but I had an agreement with Geoff that, if all went well, he would promote me to assistant director. In fact, one year later he made me his assistant.

Today, Shelly is running a large academic laboratory; Geoff is working as head of global R&D for another large multinational; and Ichiro moved to New York to run a small venture capital firm. When asked about their respective careers, each responded as follows:

*Geoff:*

I still envy people like Shelly who have made important discoveries. I ask myself: "What have you achieved?" And all I can answer is that I am a manager. Now I have to get my technical pleasures vicariously: Talking to my staff, hearing what they're up to, reading their work.

I discovered that I *like* making decisions, influencing the direction of large groups of people. I like contributing to the success of the organization in the broadest sense. I *like* being a manager. Although I'm envious sometimes when I read about what people in, say, the defense research laboratories are doing, I've long since come to terms with being a manager.

*Shelly*:

What I want to find in my research activities, whether I'm in industry or academia, is not to do whatever I please. I look for specific goals, such as "design to this tolerance." I also look for constraints and restrictions, such as "design to this tolerance, within this budget and in this time frame," because I think that is how I succeed. I have noticed that whenever people decide that no constraint is going to stand in their way, nothing does.

When I was in industry I had no idea what would be profitable, but I could say if the problem was only wishful thinking. I still cannot predict if anything coming out of my experiments will be profitable, but I can say with certainty that this is the way to tackle the problems.

*Ichiro*:

I had no career plan that involved industry, but I was becoming bored with my government job. I know that I'm a capable engineer but I'm not a very creative one. So when I moved to [the small entrepreneurial firm] I did not regard my career as going *from* science *to* management; I regarded it as a move to "science management." What I was glad to do was move out of the laboratory.

I discovered in that first industry job that what really fascinates me is having an idea about strategy and then bringing all the bits and pieces together to attain the strategy. That is what is so interesting about this venture capital organization. When you're in a job in which you can integrate and manipulate the bits and pieces and use a lot of input to make strategy happen—that's what I love.

## Analysis of Work-Related Needs

Although Shelly, Geoff, and Ichiro are about the same age, with similar backgrounds and work experience in the same company, each has a different dominant work-related need and, therefore, exhibits a different human aspect within his or her personal competencies.

Shelly exemplifies the scientist with a very high need for achievement. As you have inferred from the story, such a person sets her own goals, persists as long as it takes to reach them, and is not easily distracted ("I was happily unaware," "I just went on working . . ."). However, such a scientist must be kept *challenged* or she will leave. Both companies failed to keep Shelly "motivated" because management tried to typecast her after her success (i.e., keep her working on the development of second- and third-generation products).

Shelly loves to be the solo contributor and does not enjoy managing people other than those who work on *her* projects. She is quite uninterested in spending time dealing with "people problems."

Geoff exemplifies the scientist with a dominant need for affiliation, as evidenced by his focus on work relationships and his distress when Shelly was upset over the decision to name him manager. He was also distressed whenever he had to deal with people from that "second group" who, he knew, would be "blunt" and "outspoken." He has a secondary need for power, reflected in his statements about liking to "influence large groups of people" and in his ability to manage his bosses (persuading corporate management not to discontinue Shelly's project) and to shield his scientists from what he felt were inappropriate corporate pressures (so that Shelly was unaware of any decisions about her project).

Ichiro exemplifies the scientist with a dominant need for power. He was not happy working in a laboratory as solo contributor; he prefers to think about strategy. He is most attracted to jobs that allow him to bring "all the bits and pieces together," so that his current position as head of a venture capital firm is very exciting for him.

The dominant work-related need of each of these scientists was clear from their description of their first job in industry. Shelly recalled the equipment and the facility in which she could run her experiments. Geoff recalled the people—knowing one another no matter what one's place in the organizational hierarchy. Ichiro recalled the organization structure and then commented on his own career expectations.

Imagine that you are recruiting and you interview these scientists. To understand what motivates people, listen carefully to how they describe their experiences. What do they talk about? What do they like? What don't they like? What did they do well?

Consider Shelly. Her means–end focus is apparent (the equipment at the first corporation; the resources and technicians at the second). What is she looking for? Goals, constraints, restrictions, commitment. Why did she leave the two companies? Because she did not want to be typecast. A scientist like this will be motivated as a solo contributor if kept challenged. If you can keep the high-achievement-need scientists challenged, you can almost guarantee the technical progress of the R&D organization.

Consider Geoff. His focus on people is as apparent as Shelly's focus on things. Geoff described his first job in terms of people as well as his current job (getting his technical pleasures from "talking to people"). He also handled the difficult situation with Shelly (when he was first promoted to management) so competently that not only did she not leave immediately but she also went on to make a second important discovery. Of course, the stress of dealing with these difficult situations can take its toll physically. A scientist like this will be motivated in a position that allows him or her to focus on interpersonal relationships.

Finally, consider Ichiro. His focus on organization and strategy is apparent in his description of his first job in industry. He took over a large department very early in his industry career and was so successful that he was soon promoted to assistant director of R&D. A scientist like this will be motivated in a position that puts him or her in the "big picture" and allows scope for working on change and strategy.

## Is There a Personality "Type" That Is Recognizable?

You may be developing in your mind's eye a picture of the "high achiever," the "high power," the "high affiliator" person. There is indeed a "type," but it comes packaged in a variety of ways. There is no easy, surface, indicator of this aspect of personality. You cannot discern work motivation needs by examining only external aspects like dress and social behavior. You *can* discern work motivation needs by listening carefully to people and observing the patterns of their work behaviors over time.

## SOME MANAGEMENT IMPLICATIONS

We will be "motivated" when the basic conditions of work are met and the human aspects of our job fit the human aspects of our personality. Some of us stumble into the right job; others correctly choose the position; still others are in the right job but choose, or are moved to, one that does not suit them. When there is no longer a fit between personal competencies and job demands, the joy goes out of our work. We may delude ourselves for a time with title, prestige, or money, but fundamentally we will not be happy (motivated).

Perhaps the most common mistake made in R&D organizations is promoting a person to a management position on the basis of scientific or technical performance, without taking into account the fit (or lack of fit) between the human aspects of the job and the individual's work-related needs. If the organization is lucky, the individual discovers that managing R&D is what he or she really loves to do. Usually, however, the scientist is first pleased and then increasingly frustrated at being away from the science. Some try to maintain their bench experiments, but then both the science and the management suffer.

Scientific or technical "ladders"—titles and positions and rewards for scientists that parallel the management track but do not carry management responsibilities—may be appropriate. Of course, the parallel ladder must be just that: *parallel*. If the organization really does not value scientific and technical achievement as much as business accomplishments, then the accoutrements of the ladder are a sham. If your organization is fortunate to employ a "Shelly," and you want to keep her, then you must keep her challenged and rewarded with meaningful acknowledgements (including pay and benefits) that are visible to the entire organization.

If *you* are in the right job, and you are recruiting, consider the issue of balance in R&D. As a management rule of thumb, you want enough scientists with dominant need for achievement to ensure technical progress; several (depending on size) with dominant need for power to ensure strategic direction and focus; as well as a sufficient number of scientists with dominant need for affiliation, to function as the "glue" that keeps the organization together.

If you are managing and believe you have unmotivated scientists, consider moving them around to tasks that better fit their personal competencies. If there is no possibility, then a serious discussion of other career moves is in order, before the person becomes truly demoralized and erodes the morale of the whole organization.

If you are thinking about promoting a scientist to management and, after reflection believe that the person has a dominant need for affiliation and would enjoy the position, then consider the type of training you should provide. What will be difficult for this person at first are the decisions that hurt some people, as exemplified by Geoff's realization that he might not have been able to promote someone like himself rather than Shelly to management.

## If You Are in the Right Job, Is Your Boss?

A crucial management task is managing *up*, as well as across and down. Perhaps your boss was incorrectly promoted from the bench to management. Your job, then, requires that you "interpret" the person for your staff and perhaps for others in upper management. You might have to "think for two"; that is, take care of your own responsibilities and consider what your boss should be doing, and attempt, diplomatically, to coach and suggest. In the case of a high achiever promoted to management, you might recommend an assistant with a dominant need for affiliation and think about how strategic leadership might be provided by a team or task force that includes your boss plus someone with both the desire and the work-related need for power.

## SUMMARY

A research and development organization with highly motivated people exhibits an almost audible "hum" that can be recognized very quickly. It is an organization in which people love to work and for whom almost nothing is impossible.

In such an organization the basic conditions of work are met, and the manager of R&D works hard to ensure that the human aspects of the job and of the person are matched. People's deeper needs—for power, for achievement, and for affiliation—are addressed.

## NOTES

1. See, for example, the excellent overview of theories provided in *Organizational Behavior*, by Gregory Moorhead and Ricky W. Griffin, Boston, MA: Houghton-Mifflin, 1994.
2. The three areas of influence were described by R. E. Boyatzis, "Competence at Work," in A. J. Stewart (Ed), *Motivation and Society*, San Francisco, CA: Jossey-Bass, 1982.
3. See, for example, David McClelland's *Motives, Personality, and Society*, New York: Praeger, 1984.
4. The pictures and instructions are taken from P. P. Dawson, *Fundamentals of Organizational Behavior*, Englewood Cliffs, New Jersey: Prentice-Hall, 1985 (reprinted with permission). The scoring techniques are based on J. W. Atkinson (Ed.), *Motives in Fantasy, Action, and Society*, New York: van Nostrand, 1958.
5. This research is described in A. J. Stewart, op. cit.
6. All the stories presented in this book are composites and not meant to resemble particular persons or organizations but many people and many organizations.

# CHAPTER THREE

# UNDERSTANDING YOUR LEADERSHIP STYLE AND THAT OF OTHERS

## WHAT IS STYLE?

Leadership style is the second major human aspect of our personal competencies, as shown on the Venn diagram in Chapter 2. Like our work-related needs for power, affiliation, and achievement, our *preferred* leadership style is also a stable part of our personalities. However, management research indicates that we can and must alter our preferred or natural leadership behavior to suit the circumstances. The critical question is, of course, what style and under what circumstances? Before that question is discussed, two points must be clarified.

First, the term "leadership" means being an exemplar and inspiration to scientists in R&D, as well as directing them in a course of action, in decision-making, and in problem solving. No matter what your formal title, this chapter assumes that you have some or all of these "leadership" responsibilities.

Second, "leadership style" must be distinguished from other terms often included under the subject of leadership. For example, you may have heard someone described as an "autocratic leader" (or "democratic," or "participative"). These terms have less to do with leadership style than with how one includes or does not include input from others. *Autocratic* implies that little or no input from others is sought or used; *democratic*, that the wishes of the majority are decisive; *consensus*, that the relevant parties must agree before an action is taken; and *participative*, that wide input is sought, although the choice of action may be decided solely by the "leader."[1]

How and to what extent you include input from others should be governed by common sense. If there is a crisis, you may have no choice but to be autocratic. No one disputes the autocracy of a physician at an accident scene. If you are selecting the color of the walls in the cafeteria, then the wishes of the majority of workers should be respected. If you are not the expert in the subject at hand, you should ensure that those who are agree on the steps to be taken. And if your coworkers and subordinates will be greatly affected by the outcome, you should seek their wide participation in the process as much as possible.

The norms in your organization (discussed in the following chapter) also affect how and to what extent you include input from others. In some organizations, gaining consensus is important. In others, little participation is expected by those who lead and those who follow.

In this chapter, leadership style refers to two types of central tendencies in behavior that were observed by a well-known researcher in the field of leadership, Fred Fiedler. Fiedler noted that people tend to direct action, make decisions, and solve problems within organizations in one of two ways:[2]

- Focusing on the *task* at hand and imposing structure (e.g., procedures and methods) on that task.
- Focusing on the *people* involved in the task and working to ensure good organizational relationships.

Fiedler proposed that these central tendencies are a stable part of our personality, like our work-related needs for power, achievement, and affiliation. Each of us has a preferred or natural style, but this style or central tendency to behave in a certain way can be modified. Moreover, each style—task-focused and relationship-focused—has been found to be more effective in certain situations. In brief, a task-focused style is more effective when the action (or decision or problem) is explicit, even if uncertainty is high. For example, you are starting a project in an area of research new to the organization, although work in other organizations has indicated the project should be doable. A relationship-focused style is more effective when the action (or decision or problem) is ambiguous or equivocal. For example, you are starting a project in an entirely novel area of research in which there are multiple and conflicting interpretations of "the problem."

The explanation for the difference in effectiveness is straightforward. A task-focused style imposes structure (procedures, methods, algorithms) on a situation. If the situation is explicit, then a task-focused style improves organizational efficiency. People get the job done better and faster. But if the situation is ambiguous, imposing structure at the start will curtail the wide information-seeking and communicating activities needed to reduce ambiguity to the point that the group can move forward. In the latter situation, a focus on relationships, to ensure candid and challenging discussion, will be more effective.[3] (Some of these issues will be taken up again in Chapter 5, under organizational structure, and in Chapter 7, under project management.)

## UNDERSTANDING YOUR STYLE AND THAT OF OTHERS

**NOTICE:** This exercise, like the first, can only be completed and scored before you read the explanation and discussion below. Ensure that you have an uninterrupted 15 minutes to complete the exercise.

### Second Exercise in Managerial Wisdom

Fiedler devised a brief questionnaire that helps to identify the central tendency of behavior that is your preferred or natural leadership style. Here are the instructions: Think of a person with whom you work or have worked *least well*. You may have liked or disliked the person; what is important for the purpose of the questionnaire is that the two of you did not work well together. That is why it is called the "Least Preferred Coworker" (LPC) questionnaire. Describe the person, using the following scale (e.g., if you think of this person as "pleasant," check number 8 on the first item). Go through the material carefully; the scales reverse throughout the questionnaire.[4]

## Least Preferred Coworker (LPC) Scale

| Pleasant | 8 | 7 | 6 | 5 | 4 | 3 | 2 | 1 | Unpleasant __ |
|---|---|---|---|---|---|---|---|---|---|

| Friendly | 8 | 7 | 6 | 5 | 4 | 3 | 2 | 1 | Unfriendly __ |
|---|---|---|---|---|---|---|---|---|---|

| Rejecting | 1 | 2 | 3 | 4 | 5 | 6 | 7 | 8 | Accepting __ |
|---|---|---|---|---|---|---|---|---|---|

| Tense | 1 | 2 | 3 | 4 | 5 | 6 | 7 | 8 | Relaxed __ |
|---|---|---|---|---|---|---|---|---|---|

| Distant | 1 | 2 | 3 | 4 | 5 · 6 | 7 | 8 | Close __ |
|---|---|---|---|---|---|---|---|---|

| Cold | 1 | 2 | 3 | 4 | 5 | 6 | 7 | 8 | Warm __ |
|---|---|---|---|---|---|---|---|---|---|

| Supportive | 8 | 7 | 6 | 5 | 4 | 3 | 2 | 1 | Hostile __ |
|---|---|---|---|---|---|---|---|---|---|

| Boring | 1 | 2 | 3 | 4 | 5 | 6 | 7 | 8 | Interesting __ |
|---|---|---|---|---|---|---|---|---|---|

| Quarrelsome | 1 | 2 | 3 | 4 | 5 | 6 | 7 | 8 | Harmonious __ |
|---|---|---|---|---|---|---|---|---|---|

| Gloomy | 1 | 2 | 3 | 4 | 5 | 6 | 7 | 8 | Cheerful __ |
|---|---|---|---|---|---|---|---|---|---|

| Open | 8 | 7 | 6 | 5 | 4 | 3 | 2 | 1 | Guarded __ |
|---|---|---|---|---|---|---|---|---|---|

| Backbiting | 1 | 2 | 3 | 4 | 5 | 6 | 7 | 8 | Loyal __ |
|---|---|---|---|---|---|---|---|---|---|

| Untrustworthy | 1 | 2 | 3 | 4 | 5 | 6 | 7 | 8 | Trustworthy __ |
|---|---|---|---|---|---|---|---|---|---|

| Considerate | 8 | 7 | 6 | 5 | 4 | 3 | 2 | 1 | Unconsiderate __ |
|---|---|---|---|---|---|---|---|---|---|

| Nasty | 1 | 2 | 3 | 4 | 5 | 6 | 7 | 8 | Nice __ |
|---|---|---|---|---|---|---|---|---|---|

| Agreeable | 8 | 7 | 6 | 5 | 4 | 3 | 2 | 1 | Disagreeable __ |
|---|---|---|---|---|---|---|---|---|---|

| Insincere | 1 | 2 | 3 | 4 | 5 | 6 | 7 | 8 | Sincere __ |
|---|---|---|---|---|---|---|---|---|---|

| Kind | 8 | 7 | 6 | 5 | 4 | 3 | 2 | 1 | Unkind __ |
|---|---|---|---|---|---|---|---|---|---|

Total __

*Transfer your scale position number to the scoring column.

When you have finished, sum your answers for your total score (which will be between 18 and 144). If your total score was between 18 and 57, you have a central tendency to be a *task-focused leader*. If your score was between 64 and 144, you have a central tendency to be a *relationship-focused leader*. (If you scored between 58 and 63, pick the endpoint to which you are closer.)

Note that the high scores on the questionnaire reflect a positive assessment of your least preferred coworker. If you describe this person in positive terms, your preferred style is relationship-focused. If you describe this person in negative terms (with low scores), your preferred style is task-focused.

Again, short of becoming an expert in administering and interpreting the LPC questionnaire, what can you do to understand better the preferred leadership style of others? You can listen to them and observe them, using the insights you have gained from reflecting on your own style. The analysis of the following story about two scientists, each with a distinct leadership style, will also be helpful.[5]

## Two Leadership Styles

Lee and Stefan are physicists who direct nationally renowned research facilities. Each made the transition to R&D management in a different way:

*Lee:*

> The big transition for me was moving from chief of particle physics to director of this institute. As chief, I ran a relatively small facility of about $0.5 million per year. Then the director of the institute became ill, and

I was asked to apply for the job. I took a month to decide. While I bicycled back and forth to work I would ask why I wanted to take on a budget of nearly $200 million and a lot more management responsibilities. My family became tired of listening to my arguments!

*Stefan:*

My transition to management was more gradual. I started out as a post-doc in another university, gradually became responsible for a group of doctoral students and technicians, and then became assistant professor and chief of the laser laboratory. This involved a certain amount of managerial responsibility—if nothing else, worrying about the performance of my staff. I gradually took on more responsibilities, ultimately becoming director of the entire department.

When asked what advice they might offer other scientists facing similar career choices, they responded:

*Lee:*

First of all, you should move into management sooner rather than later. I think that when you are new to management you have all kinds of ideas you'll try out, because you're not embedded in the bureaucracy. The older you get, the more entangled you become in "the system" and you start to accept it at face value. That's why my first point is "do it now."

My second point is, if you want to have influence over the way an organization is run and over where it is going, take a management job. When I was offered the job of director of this institute, there were a lot of things I thought could be improved. It seemed to me to be a good opportunity to make changes I believed were important.

*Stefan:*

Of course, those are good points, but there are other considerations. You should reflect on the issue of whether you will grieve at being away from the bench. I spend a lot of time with people in my department who are thinking about this, telling them that if they are not absolutely sure they can leave research without a terrible sense of loss, they should not go into management.

Moreover, too often people decide to take a management position because work is not going well in the laboratory, or they disagree with their department chair, or they didn't get tenure. Something of that sort. But moving into management should be a positive step. If you're a manager only by default, you will never be effective.

Both Lee and Stefan are very successful managers who gave these reasons for their success:

*Lee:*

I believe very strongly that, to be good at a job like this, you have to stay very close to the science. I hold a weekly session that is required attendance for our institute's management committee. We invite a very select group of physicists who are on the leading edge or who are controversial. This allows us to judge where we should invest our money.

I also believe it's crucial to the success of the institute that I hire the brightest person I can possibly find. I've watched a number of my colleagues hire people they feel they can get along with. And, we have to admit, we sometimes feel most comfortable with people who have to look up to us. I've always tried to hire the smartest possible person, even though I have had some problems and my hires have not always worked out.

*Stefan:*

I agree about hiring the best and the smartest because people are, as far as I'm concerned, the most precious resource I have. I try to choose staff carefully, to nurture them, to be in communication with them. I think this is the most important aspect of managing scientists.

Whom I hire, how I mentor them, and where I place them are crucial. If my staff is incapable of doing something, or doesn't trust me, or doesn't care enough to do it well, then the work of this department is not going to be accomplished satisfactorily. Anything that is done well is done because there are good scientists to do it.

When asked about their management styles, Lee and Stefan gave these examples:

*Lee:*

Two years ago a very highly regarded scientist needed a larger space and more responsibility, or he would have left the institute. At the time, there was a department in another one of our buildings that really didn't belong in that building. In a very swift maneuver, I decided to move his entire corridor, and we created a laboratory for this other scientist in its place. That person now is one of my division directors.

The other scientist, the one I moved out, barely

**49**

spoke to me for months because he was very angry. But when his laboratory began to flourish in its new location, because it was surrounded by others engaged in very complementary research, he came to me and said he thought I did the right thing.

*Stefan:*

I have scientists working for me who are very eccentric and yet very brilliant. When I am asked where I draw the line when they cause trouble, I say that I draw the line very far away. I try to keep these eccentric scientists from getting into trouble in the first place. But I understand what they're like and I understand that, if I don't have people like that, I will have a very mediocre institution.

One of our scientists has required a lot of my understanding over the years. He has made people very angry because of his arrogance, but I stood between them and him. Now I take particular satisfaction in his enormous scientific achievements.

How do they feel about managing a scientific enterprise?

*Stefan:*

You have to be willing to give up the satisfactions of your own research and to get that satisfaction by helping with someone else's. You become a facilitator, and then you can begin to discern some progress in the field of physics. But you have to be able to take satisfaction from the *facilitation* instead of the experimental work itself.

Managing R&D is much less visible and less easily viewed as success than managing an organization that produces some tangible output. I have had to look for the many small ways in which I can find satisfaction, such as my day-to-day working with people, not just in the spectacular accomplishments they sometimes achieve.

*Lee:*

Often, the manager of R&D is simply not recognized. That's hard, because I have an ego like everybody else. The hardest part of this job for me was realizing that, by the time the world recognized my influence, I would be old and gray!

## Analysis of Leadership Styles

Just as you should be able to recognize work-related needs for power, achievement, and affiliation from what people say and how they view their work, so too should you be able to recognize that Lee has a task-focused and Stefan a relationship-focused leadership style. Consider how each viewed their transition to management. Lee talked about the difference in budget (i.e., *structure*) between the respective organizations; Stefan about increasing responsibilities for people (i.e., *relationships*).

In advising other scientists about management, each responded to the issue in a manner consistent with her or his style. Lee put structure around the decision: do it sooner rather than later, and do it if you want to make changes. Stefan recommended that the person first reflect about "grieving" for the lack of bench involvement and said he spent "a lot of time with people," counseling them about this career move. In other words, he focused on relationships.

*51*

When each was asked why they were successful, Lee talked about staying close to the science and hiring the brightest people. Stefan said that people were the most important resource for the organization and that management must "nurture them and be in close communication with them."

Finally, when asked to give an example of their management style, Lee described her imposition of structure on the situation regarding her "very highly regarded scientist" (moving a corridor of people to another building). But Stefan described those scientists whom he strives to "understand" and to protect from others who might have less patience with their eccentricity.

Do you think your style is closer to Lee's or to Stefan's?

As you read this story, did you also consider that Lee probably has a dominant need for power? Like Ichiro in the story in Chapter 2, Lee speaks about the organization and her position, about taking charge and making changes. Stefan, on the other hand, probably has a dominant need for affiliation. Like Geoff in Chapter 2, Stefan speaks primarily about nurturing and mentoring people and protecting those whose eccentricity makes them vulnerable to criticism.

Because they are both part of our personality, there is an association between our ordering of work-related needs (McClelland's theory) and our preferred leadership style (Fiedler's theory).[6] If you have a very high need for achievement, your questionnaire score is likely to be between 18 and 57. If you have a very high need for affiliation, your questionnaire score is likely to be between 64 and 144 (probably in the 80s or 90s). If your dominant need and score do not match, then it is probable that your leadership score will match your secondary need.

The association between work-related needs and leadership style will also give you some sense of the "distance" between your primary or dominant and secondary needs. For example, if you determined that your ordering of motivation needs were power → affiliation → achievement and your score were high (e.g., 100 or more), then your need for affiliation would be very "close" to your dominant need of power. If your score were low (e.g., 48), then the "distance" between power and affiliation would be large, but the "distance" between affiliation and achievement would be small. If your ordering of motivation needs were affiliation → achievement → power and your score were low, then achievement would be "close" to your dominant need, and so forth.

On that basis, look at your graphic description of your motivation needs and adjust it, using your leadership style score. Think about this in light of the discussion in Chapter 2.

## SOME MANAGEMENT IMPLICATIONS

If your preferred leadership style is task-focused, it will be more effective when the action, issue, or problem is explicit. But, you must exercise caution when the circumstances are different. If, as in the examples noted earlier, your group were beginning research in a novel area, you would have to be careful not to impose structure too soon. Rather, you should ensure wide and challenging communication among those involved, to reduce equivocality, by ensuring good interpersonal relationships. When the ambiguity was reduced to the point that there was agreement about the problem, then your task-focused style would be more effective.

Similarly, if your preferred leadership style is relationship-focused, it will be more effective when the action, issue, or problem is ambiguous. Your preferred style will serve you well in the above example of beginning research in a novel area. But you must exercise caution and not persevere in emphasizing relationships when the ambiguity of the problem is reduced. At that point, you must modify your behavior and your style to be task-focused and impose structure so the job can be completed efficiently.

Of course, work is rarely so clear-cut. You will, in fact, need to reflect on the explicitness/ambiguity of all the situations you face as manager. In the beginning, you will probably "lapse" into your preferred style and only later reflect on its effectiveness. Soon, you will not respond until you have first thought about the situation. Finally, you will develop, through practice and reflection and learning from your mistakes, a facility for matching your style to the requirements of the situation.

You also have to identify the preferred leadership style of your boss and manage situations in which your boss' style is not effective. Similarly, if you are considering one of your scientists for a management position and have concluded that this would be a good fit in terms of that person's work-related needs, you must also identify that person's leadership style. How does this scientist approach a situation? By imposing structure, or by emphasizing relationships? Once you have recognized that central tendency in behavior, your mentoring should include providing guidance about when and why each leadership style is effective, as well as providing a clear and persuasive example by your own actions.

## IN SUMMARY

One hallmark of effective leadership is the ability to adjust one's preferred leadership style to the requirements of the situation. When the action, decision, or problem requiring leadership is explicit, the more effective style is to focus on the task at hand and to impose structure on that task. But when the action or decision or problem requiring leadership is ambiguous, the more effective style is to focus on the people involved and to ensure good relationships among those engaged in the task until the ambiguity is reduced.

Understanding your preferred style, its strengths and limitations, is an important step in becoming an effective leader of R&D.

# NOTES

1. The interested reader should also review the many theories on leadership in, for example, Gregory Moorhead and Ricky W. Griffin's *Organizational Behavior*, Boston, MA: Houghton-Mifflin, 1994.
2. Fiedler's leadership style model is discussed in the above text.
3. This aspect of leadership is addressed in a number of studies of group problem-solving performance, beginning with the early study, *Human Information Processing*, by H. M. Schroder, M. Driver, and S. Streufert, New York: Holt, Rinehart and Winston, 1967.
4. The questionnaire and instructions are taken from *Fundamentals of Organizational Behavior*, Peter P. Dawson, Prentice-Hall, Englewood Cliffs, NJ, 1985, reprinted with permission.
5. This case study is a composite and not meant to reflect particular people or organizations but rather many people and many organizations.
6. For the past several years the author has been informally tracking the McClelland TAT results and Fiedler LPC scores of executive (scientists) and graduate (Master's students) classes. Although this is not meant to be rigorous research, with very few exceptions the needs and scores match as described in the text.

# DISCERNING AND ASSESSING ORGANIZATIONAL CULTURE

Organizational culture shares at least two attributes with individual personality: 1) both have a profound impact on the work environment, and 2) both are very difficult to change. This chapter focuses on the first attribute (Chapter 9 focuses on the second).

Culture is the major human aspect of the organizational characteristics sphere in the Venn diagram presented in Chapter 2. As discussed in that chapter, ensuring a match between 1) the technical and human aspects of the job demands and 2) the technical and human aspects of your and your scientists' personal competencies is required for an energetic and enthusiastic ("motivated") R&D organization. Achieving an energetic, enthusiastic, and *creative* group of scientists requires that organizational characteristics—the third sphere—support collaboration, intellectual challenge, candid and transparent communication, and willingness to take risks. Unless both the human and technical aspects of the larger social context support these qualities, novel science and technology cannot emerge.[1]

This chapter presents a model of organizational culture, to help you discern the culture of your organization and assess how that culture either fosters or inhibits scientific creativity. Chapter 5 discusses the major technical aspects of the organization—structure, size, and formal systems—required to support novel science and technology.

## A MODEL OF CULTURE

Culture, like personality, can be described as a "layered" phenomenon consisting of three levels: manifestations, justifications, and core.[2]

## Manifestations

The outer level of culture consists, first, of such tangible manifestations as the formal logo or symbol of the organization found on stationery and business cards; the physical facilities (especially headquarters or the equivalent); the geographic site(s) of the facilities; dress codes; and the like.

Second, informal symbols also manifest culture. In many organizations there is an image that is widely held as illustrative of what the organization is really like. For example, one R&D facility was described by its scientists as a "chemical fortress." Not surprisingly, efforts to introduce different technologies were extraordinarily difficult. Another was depicted as a longboat in which alternating oars faced in opposite directions. The scientists (those at the oars) felt that, though they pulled energetically, there was no agreement on or movement toward a coherent direction.

Third, intangible behaviors manifest culture, such as rituals around:

- meetings (having food or not, arriving late, arriving promptly, seating arrangements, etc.)
- decision-making (seeking wide input, rarely asking for input, gaining consensus, etc.; see Chapter 3)
- communicating (going only through channels, circumventing channels, relying on the grapevine, using E-mail, not using E-mail, etc.; see Chapter 6)
- eating (at one's desk, in the lunchroom with one's discipline colleagues, sharing food among the team, etc.)
- socializing, and so on.

## Justifications

Below this surface level, the next layer of culture consists of the reasons or justifications people give for organizational actions, either directly in response to questions or indirectly in formal communications. Justifications may be found in published documents, such as annual reports ("We decided to invest in X because . . . "); brochures ("Our organization is committed to Y because . . . "); newsletters ("You will have noticed that we changed Z because . . . ").

They are also found in the stories that make up organizational traditions handed on to new employees or repeated under certain circumstances (like success or crisis). For example, development engineers in a mid-sized European software company explained that their emphasis on family, especially their quiet and polite way of dealing with each other, derived from the death-bed wish of the company's founder. According to tradition, this man gathered his seven direct reports around his bed and admonished them: "Never fight with one another."

## Core Ideology[3]

The most important part of culture is the core or deepest level. At the core are a few, key beliefs about those fundamental qualities that embody, for members, the organization's very reason for being. These beliefs affect the warp and weft of organizational life and are at the root of assumptions rarely questioned by organizational members (but often reflected in the *justifications* or second level of culture). The three layers or levels of culture are connected, but the direction of influence is from the core out. Both the surface manifestations and the justifications for organizational action provide only clues. To understand the culture, you must understand the core.

The core ideology emerges from the founding history of the organization, including the experiences and background of the founder(s). It is forged in the early successes and crises of the organization. As Edgar Schein noted, if the organization prospers, then people will "repeat what works and give up what does not." If there are failures, then "once people learn how to avoid a painful situation, they continue to pursue this course."[4]

Culture—the core ideology—has been described as a handbook for organizational survival, which makes it extremely powerful.[5] People learn that their "survival" quite literally depends on holding certain beliefs and modeling certain behaviors, like the politeness noted above. Moreover, core beliefs act like lenses through which people in the organization "see" the world. If these beliefs are interpreted in a way that is incongruent with the qualities required for scientific creativity, then the core ideology acts like astigmatism in a lens, a source of distortion. Such distortions are difficult for those in the organization to examine and recognize, however. And, because they are linked with survival, they are difficult to challenge once they are recognized. That is why culture is so hard to change.

The core ideology that evolves from shared history is handed on to generations of organizational members by at least three means. First, newcomers to the organization tend to imitate other members and, by that means, come to share their beliefs. Second, job tasks provide a means for people to talk together and come to a shared understanding of "the world" as viewed through the lenses of the core beliefs. Finally, 1) hiring policies (often described in terms of finding people who "fit" the organization), 2) formal training, 3) job descriptions, 4) apprenticeships, 5) mentorships, and 6) all the formal and informal means by which organizational members convey appropriate language and behaviors to new members also transmit the core ideology.

To help you understand how core ideology emerges and the potential impact of culture on R&D, three annotated illustrations are provided. The first is the story of "Jensen A/S."[6]

# AN ILLUSTRATION OF CULTURE: JENSEN A/S

## Founding History

Ole Jensen Arnoldsson, a Swedish chemist, moved to Denmark around 1850 and settled in what was then farmland north of Copenhagen. He went to Copenhagen University and completed a doctorate in organic chemistry, married, and began to work as the first research chemist in a local fertilizer manufacturing company. The couple had five children, all of whom were sent to the university, and three (two sons and a daughter) went on to receive their PhDs in chemistry.

After completing their doctorates, sons Henry and Stig joined their father as company researchers. Shortly thereafter, Henry discovered a novel method for producing high-quality chemicals and, at the age of 34, decided to form a partnership with his brother. They named their company "Jensen" and set up operations in what was formerly a large outbuilding of one of the local dairy farms.

Jensen prospered and, by the turn of the century, was producing fine chemicals that were used throughout Scandinavia. Henry's insistence on "quality foremost" was understood to be one of the reasons for Jensen's success, and this slogan was printed on all the stationery and labels used by the company.

Henry was president of Jensen for 35 years, and three of his seven children also worked in and then took over the family business when he retired. He had the foresight to build one of the first research departments in the fine-chemicals industry, and he oversaw the expansion of sales to Europe and then to Asia. Overshadowing his business and scientific acumen, however, was his reputation for paternalism. Even before Jensen was profitable, and before it became standard practice, Henry allowed employees to leave work early on Saturday and shortened the work week to 35 hours (at full pay) during July and August. Like his father before him, Henry was active in the cultural and political life of the community, donating money to build schools and hospitals, support the symphony, and expand the museum. He also served nearly 20 years in local government.

In 1935, Henry's middle son became president of Jensen, and the tradition of Jensen family leadership continued into the 1950s, when the company went public (Jensen A/S). From the time of its founding, all employees were on salary, and no one was ever laid off. In a company history written in the 1970s, the Jensen's were praised as a prominent local family who, unlike other corporate founders, did not move away to become absentee landlords of their company facilities.

By the 1970s, Jensen's products were known for their high quality and the company was known for its dependability. Sales of fine chemicals formed the mainstay of the corporation and accounted for nearly $1 billion by 1975. At that time the company expanded into additional international markets and became organized by product line for the end customer (e.g., food, perfumes, leather, etc.).

## Core Ideology

This very brief founding history suggests that at least three beliefs might constitute the core ideology of Jensen's culture: belief in education, belief in quality, and belief in family. Such beliefs can be very positive in any organization, depending on how they are interpreted. A belief in education can be interpreted as valuing highly trained scientists and intellectual achievement. A belief in quality can be interpreted as valuing excellence of organizational output, quality of product as well as quality of science behind the product. And a belief in family can be interpreted as valuing humane regard for all workers.

But these beliefs can also be interpreted in such a way as to inhibit collaboration, intellectual challenge, candid and transparent communication, and willingness to take risks—the organizational qualities required for scientific creativity. At Jensen, the belief in education instead became a rationale for a quasi-academic research organization in which the need for novel products, on which the company ultimately depended, was complacently deemphasized in favor of "good science." The belief in quality, and Henry's slogan was still printed on all company labels, had become a rationale for time-consuming and risk-averse decision making. Finally, the belief in family and paternalism had been interpreted to mean one's superior knows best, challenge is not respectful, and being nice (at least to one's face) is most important.

Paternalism also kept Jensen headquarters and R&D facility in a small town in Denmark, although most similar companies are now located in larger European countries and in the U.S. Jensen's relative isolation made it difficult to recruit leading-edge scientists, many of whom chose to work closer to the universities at which major discoveries were being made. But the company had originally prospered with these beliefs, and employees kept repeating "what works" even a century later, as the Taiwan decision, below, demonstrates.

## The Taiwan Decision

Jensen had set up a sales office in Taiwan in the late 1930s and had added a small laboratory for onsite testing of chemicals to be sold there. Because of the potential size of the Asian market, the company sent a research chemist from Denmark, in the mid-1970s, to conduct a feasibility study of expanding this small laboratory to a full-sized R&D facility. The chemist discovered that the current location would not be suitable for expansion, and Jensen managers had to decide whether to build in another location in Taiwan, to expand the Danish facility, or to build an R&D facility elsewhere in Europe or in the U.S.

Under the direction of the vice president of research and development, Steen Tastrup, a study team was sent to Taiwan in 1982. The team concluded that a full-scale R&D

facility should be built at another location in Taiwan. By 1986, a site had been chosen and the construction begun.

In a 1988 conversation between the manager of the new Taiwan laboratory, Ib Dissing, and Steen Tastrup, the justifications for the Taiwan decision were stated to be as follows:

*Steen*:

We considered locating a facility in Germany, and we considered the U.S. Because Asia is one of our biggest markets, we decided that the best way to meet their needs was to build a research facility there.

*Ib*:

In addition to the commercial aspects, we decided that building in Taiwan would open new doors to a different approach to the science. And, because we would open up a new network of scientific institutions, we might also be aware, earlier, of innovations useful to our business.

I think there are two key reasons for deciding to build up an R&D presence in Taiwan. First, we want to be a global company rather than a Danish company doing business in Asia. Second, I believe we need to be open to different inputs and a different way of thinking about our science.

Such justifications for organizational action are logical, given the industry. Notice, however, how long it has taken for people at Jensen to make this decision. The initial report was sent to headquarters in the mid-1970s; a team was sent to Taiwan in 1982; and a site was chosen in 1986—almost a decade later. In comparison with its competitors, Jensen was very late in adopting a global strategy, as Steen and Ib implied:

*Steen*:

More than a decade ago we considered opening a German R&D facility. [The company had not built one at this time.] So, we have a history of responding to external forces. But that should not be confused with the strategic thinking that led us to build a laboratory in Taiwan.

*Ib*:

This time we decided to be at the forefront of internationalization in our industry. We decided to be a little bit more risk taking.

With regard to being "a little bit more risk taking," Ib continued that he saw himself as an advocate for "culture shock" within the company:

*Ib*:

To some degree, I have taken on the role of exposing Jensen to healthy culture shock. I have always said to Steen that we needed some culture shock, and I was also very vocal about efficient size in R&D. I find that, as our organization gets bigger, our bureaucracy gets bigger. We need multiple copies of reports, decisions take longer, and creativity declines.

Well, creativity declines perhaps not so much because of size as because of culture. I think that our top management have become more formal and remote, and scientists are pressured to deliver formal proposals for new research efforts.

I would say, and Steen agrees, that the culture shock of Taiwan is important to us at this juncture. If we go to Germany or the U.S., we go after every other fine-chemical company has expanded there. Jensen has been very conservative. We wait and see how others fare before we decide to follow suit.

As Steen went on to describe how management at Jensen had come to make the Taiwan decision, he revealed much about the way in which their core beliefs had actually been interpreted:

*Steen:*

We talked a lot about what type of organization we wanted Jensen to be and how big a research facility we could manage. Year after year, we would test ideas in our own R&D organization and in forums with corporate management. After a while the ideas that first appeared so startling and different began to have a certain familiarity, like your favorite slippers. I describe this as a breaking-in process, breaking in your favorite slippers. Soon, everyone is comfortable with the decision.

This is what strategic planning is all about. You have to involve people, and you have to create scenarios that have no surprises. Everyone should believe the decision was their own idea and be familiar with all of the elements. Everyone in Jensen has talked about the idea of a Taiwan laboratory many, many times over the past few years.

What is important for you to notice is that, in the same conversation, these scientists discussed the need for "culture shock" at Jensen *and* the "breaking-in," surprise-free process of making decisions. But the contradiction was not apparent to them, because they saw the world through the lenses of their core ideology.

A similar contradiction between what they intended to do (the justification) and what they might actually do was revealed in their discussion of the relationship between the Taiwan laboratory and the Danish headquarters. In the following dialogue, note the influence ("lens") of their belief in paternalism.

First, Ib stated that the two facilities must be independent, to ensure the challenge of "a different input and a different way of thinking about our science:"

*Ib*:

We realized that we could not just build a satellite laboratory in Taiwan, or we would miss the different way of thinking and different approach to the science that we needed. So, we will have Denmark and Taiwan evaluating each other, as peers, according to the expertise of the relevant scientists.

Then, Steen used the image of parent and child, revealing that the independence of the Taiwan facility, and the needed intellectual challenge at Jensen, might be difficult to achieve:

*Steen*:

Denmark is the home, the parent, and the Taiwan facility will be built to serve all of the children. But none of the children is designed to serve the global market except Taiwan.

Other research scientists at Jensen pointed to the company's problems. They realized they were coming to "diminishing returns to scale in Denmark—more money invested in R&D with less return." And they also admitted that they were anomalous in the industry by remaining in Denmark. As one chemist noted:

> To me, the strategic question is: How do we turn a company that's based in a small town in Denmark into one that truly has a global perspective?

She, too, was concerned that the Taiwan facility might not remain independent:

> Our organizational challenge will be: Do we stamp out a carbon copy of the Denmark facility, or do we build something radically different? We have to be careful not to develop the attitude that the Taiwan laboratory is an extension of the one here. We have to be careful that our R&D people don't over-control the scientists in Taiwan.

In a statement that reveals much about how "paternalism" had been interpreted, one group manager commented:

> Jensen invites you into the family and makes you captive. It's a nice company, a good company to work for. Sometimes I wonder, though, if you can't be smart *and* nice.

Ib Dissing left the following week for Taiwan. Sometime later (1991) he recounted:

*Ib*:

Senior management in Denmark have been very wary of letting scientists come over to Taiwan and of allowing open and free discussion between the two groups. I've been working very hard to loosen that. *Decisions* must go through the proper channels, but *discussion* should not be inhibited by our organizational chart.

## Jensen Today

Jensen's was known as a solid company ("dependable") in the industry, and its scientists were respected for good work. But analysts began to be concerned in the early 1980s about the company's ability to remain profitable without novel products. Although Jensen had two or three successful lines, both the process and the product technologies were mature, and customers were moving to new offerings from competing firms.

Jensen's core ideology was, in fact, inhibiting scientific creativity. The company had no new products in the "pipeline" because collaboration, intellectual challenge, candid and transparent communication, and willingness to take risks (in managing as well as in science) were not supported. Collaboration was not encouraged, as evidenced by Ib's statement about the wariness of managers to let Danish scientists spend time in Taiwan. There was little intellectual challenge, because challenge was not considered "nice." Communication was through channels, and candid assessment of the organization was seen as lack of loyalty to the company. Finally, risk aversion was pervasive in their managerial ("breaking in") processes and scientific decision making. One Swiss university professor, who had attempted to collaborate with Jensen scientists, commented about this:

I think their scientists are very, very careful, very good, extremely high quality, nothing sloppy. They pay a great deal of attention to quality control. But they move extremely slowly in research and development. It's a strange culture, though. They close the laboratories early in the summer. Also, because they are located in a rural environment, that slows them down even more. It takes them *forever* to move.

Today, Jensen A/S is on the list of possible acquisition candidates by more profitable companies. In a not-unfamiliar tactic, Steen and Ib were replaced as managers, but their successors also left after a short time. Another Jensen family member has been appointed president, and the company's reports speak confidently that Jensen can remain independent. Throughout the industry, however, scientists who are concerned about the creativity of their own research and development will say: "We don't want to become another Jensen."

# TWO FURTHER ILLUSTRATIONS OF CULTURE

Not in every organization are managers unaware that culture may be inhibiting scientific creativity. In contrast to Jensen, managers at a British telecommunications firm, "Heuris-Dahl," engaged in a rigorous assessment of their organizational culture (with outside assistance) and came to some sobering conclusions.

## Heuris-Dahl plc

In 1990, following an in-depth analysis of their organization and their position in the industry, the chairman of the board of Heuris-Dahl told employees that the company must, in order to survive in the twenty-first century, be characterized by:

- speedy research and development,
- flexible and cost-effective processes throughout the organization,
- more strategic thinking, and
- radically new products.

These statements, of course, reflected the problems the organization faced: slow research and development, rigid and cost-ineffective processes, short-range thinking, and a dearth of advanced new products.

The major reason for these problems was determined to be the company's culture. One top manager recounted:

We discovered that, although our culture supported quality, you would *never* find customer orientation, profit, or cost-effectiveness treated as a value! Now, we try to keep the value of quality and bring in the other elements.

The head of worldwide R&D, who came to the company in 1991, described what he observed in research (compare his statements with the situation at Jensen):

Heuris-Dahl had an academic ideology, a university culture. People in R&D focused on "good science" without regard for its cost or commercial applications.

Scientists used to refer to the company as "paradise." They gave you wonderful facilities and money and left you to do what you liked. You had everything you needed and no pressure at all. It was fantastic.

Complicating the situation at Heuris-Dahl (and a consequence of their founding circumstances) was the presence of
a very strong and very independent U.S. division. The head
of worldwide R&D also noted:

The U.S. felt themselves to be very powerful as far as
the corporation was concerned, because we had left
them alone. Relations between the two were getting
very strained. The U.S. and British divisions were so
independent as to be almost two separate companies.

One of the fundamental beliefs at the core of its culture
was *autonomy*, which emerged from the founding history
and, especially, the first president who, like Henry Jensen,
was in office for more than 30 years.

The first president of Heuris-Dahl, a PhD metallurgist,
was described as having organized the British company
with such a strong hand that he even oversaw the building
of headquarters and manufacturing facilities in a uniform
architectural style.

At the outbreak of World War II, the president moved
himself and top management to the U.S., and there he built
up a replica of the British facility. He personally appointed
all the heads of the foreign subsidiaries that he established,
but gave these general managers complete autonomy in
running their business. This belief in autonomy was interpreted through the years as keeping not only the divisions
but also every function at "arm's length" from corporate
management as well as from each other. It was not surprising that the U.S. division, which the president had set up
and managed during the war, acted like a "separate company." Moreover, as recently as 1992 the president of Heuris-Dahl had more than 40 general managers reporting directly to him.

The two R&D facilities were managed as autonomous

functions, with little connection to the marketplace. They were so independent, in fact, that a central research facility, nearly half the size of the British organization and on the same site, was set up to explore new technologies that the original group chose not to explore. There arose, in essence, two separate and autonomous research units in Great Britain as well as the autonomous research unit in the U.S. Their isolation from each other and from the marketplace allowed R&D to develop an "academic ideology." And, the autonomy also discouraged collaboration across organizational lines.

Since their assessment of organizational culture, employees in Heuris-Dahl have been engaged in efforts to reinterpret their core beliefs, especially autonomy, in a way consistent with the realities of the environment and consistent with the qualities required for scientific creativity. According to the head of worldwide R&D:

I have had to put in a lot of personal time trying to demonstrate from my behavior and presence that assessing research from both scientific and commercial perspectives is vital to the success of the company. I am also trying to work with the U.S. as an international organization should, collaborating and reviewing research programs together. We're also being more critical of one another, which I think is healthy.

In contrast to Jensen A/S, Heuris-Dahl has improved from number 17 in the global industry in 1985 to number 9 in 1994. They have also made several large acquisitions that improve their competitive ability, and they are especially sensitive to their cultural propensity for allowing these acquisitions to slip to "arm's length" from corporate management.

# The Cardiology Institute

The final illustration of organizational culture is a university research institute, The Cardiology Institute, that was founded in the late 1970s by a renowned academic physician, "Herman Broadbent," who had made an important discovery in the genetic components of heart disease.

Broadbent's education had been within the university in which the institute was located, and he steadfastly refused to seek scientists outside that system. Moreover, he had a very definite plan for the institute's research and tolerated no disagreement with his plan. By 1986, in the fast-moving field of molecular biology, other universities were also doing leading-edge genetic research, and The Cardiology Institute began to fall behind in the field. By 1990, when Broadbent retired, research at the institute was considered adequate but not outstanding.

Olivia Ben-David, who was recruited from another university to turn around this situation, described what she found:

Herman was very formal. He emphasized the orderliness of the institute's activities rather than individual creativity. By the time he retired, the organization was very rigid. The human touch had almost disappeared, and pressure was put on the scientists for short-term results.

Olivia's approach to the problem of culture was simple and straightforward. She recruited widely and encouraged interaction among the scientists by two means: meetings and parties. As one of the new post-doctoral fellows discovered:

There is a lot of interchange in our laboratory, and it is very egalitarian. We have breaks on Friday afternoon and the head of the laboratory brings in beer and food and we have a party. That seems typical for people here who work together to socialize as well.

There is also a fair amount of interaction among the laboratories and among departments. There are monthly department parties and weekly journal clubs. Also, I'm forced to be sociable with people from the other laboratories, because I need to use their equipment!

I was attracted to this institute because it has a growing reputation for innovation. Olivia encourages everyone who works here to try out every idea, no matter how high the risk of failure. People who are more risk taking, I believe, are more likely to be creative.

These three stories—about Jensen, Heuris-Dahl, and the Cardiology Institute—are not meant to provide an exhaustive illustration of organizational culture but rather some guideposts to help you think about your own organization. Are there characteristics of your organization that are similar to any of the above? If you reflect on the founding circumstances of your organization, can you discern problems in how the core beliefs may have been interpreted? Do capable scientists not produce the innovations you and they desire?

The next section describes why and how organizational culture can fail to allow novel science and technology to emerge.

## WHY AND HOW ORGANIZATIONAL CULTURE "FAILS"

It is ironic, and important for you to understand, that the thread joining the three illustrative organizations is *success*.

Jensen initially succeeded under Henry's direction with a core ideology encompassing quasiacademic research (education), time-consuming and risk-averse decision making (quality), and suppression of challenge (paternalism). Heuris-Dahl initially succeeded under the first president's direction with a core ideology encompassing arm's-length organizational relationships (autonomy). And The Cardiology Institute initially succeeded under Broadbent's direction with a core ideology encompassing rigid methodologies (orderliness).

As noted earlier in this chapter, when people learn that success is dependent on a certain set of beliefs and behaviors—their handbook for survival—then they keep on repeating (as Edgar Schein noted) "what works." In none of the organizations, however, did people value learning; which is to say, none valued experimenting with other ways of doing and other ways of thinking, nor did they value a rigorous assessment of their own assumptions by means of systematic feedback. As the world changed, members of these organizations continued to view it through the lenses of the core beliefs that had undergirded their initial success. They continued to behave as usual.

In all three organizations, people were hired because they fitted that particular belief system. Interviewing weeded out most of those who were "eccentric" in comparison with the desired type, and competent "eccentrics" who were hired soon left or gave up trying to change what they initially perceived as the problems in research. Even in Jensen's Taiwan facility, Ib Dissing had managed to find people who fitted the Danish mold, thus making it unlikely that he could ever bring about "culture shock."

In many organizations, initial success and homogenization by means of recruiting and hiring policies result in scientists who talk mainly to each other; who too quickly dismiss challenge, if they even really seek it from those deemed "eccentric"; who are only partially aware of the turbulence of the external environment and the consequences for their organization; and who become more and more risk averse at the same time as they complacently assure themselves they are engaged in highly uncertain (i.e., novel) research.

In the three example organizations, the qualities required for novel science and technology were not valued, or they were given only lip service. There was little or no collaboration across disciplines, at the "interstices" of the science; little or no intellectual challenge from those who could be counted upon to bring a radically different way of thinking; little or no candid and transparent communication, often under the guise of valuing civility; and no genuine risk taking, often under the guise of valuing quality.

For all three, only crises brought the possibility of self-assessment (although, at this date, there is still no evaluation underway at Jensen). But the warning signs, including loss of customers, too few innovative products in the "pipeline" of R&D, lagging ability to get products to the market in a timely and cost-effective manner, increasing inability to attract the best people, and external reputations for adequacy rather than brilliance, were clear before the crisis.

It is not that culture actually fails, of course. It is that people interpret the original core beliefs in a way counter to the qualities required for creativity, and they fail to discern that that is happening.

If you are concerned with the performance of R&D despite the qualifications of your scientists, and you believe you have a motivated group of scientists, then the problem may be with the core ideology of your organization. Addressing this problem requires that you analyze past and recent history and reflect on whether the core beliefs support or hinder scientific creativity. Changing those beliefs and behaviors is discussed in Chapter 9.

## SUMMARY

When culture "works," people collaborate because norms encourage them to ask questions of anyone, anywhere. Organizational norms also encourage intellectual challenge, reflected in impassioned arguments about principles and techniques. Communication is open and everything, including criticism, comes "straight."

An atmosphere of questioning and collaboration, of challenge and candor is by definition an atmosphere in which risk taking is encouraged. And, as the post-doctoral fellow at The Cardiology Institute noted, people who take more risks are also more likely to be creative. In such an atmosphere, novel science and technology can emerge.

Such a culture is not achieved more easily in an academic or public institution than a commercial one, nor is it more likely to be found in small rather than large organizations. As Ib Dissing stated, scientific creativity declined at Jensen "not so much because of size as because of culture." (However, as the following chapter will address, organizational structure, size, and formal systems must also be consistent with the qualities for innovation.)

One of the tasks of the effective leader of R&D is to evaluate whether the core beliefs shared by organizational members support the qualities required for scientific creativity. If they do not, then changing culture must begin with insight into the incongruities between what is encouraged in the organization and those requisite qualities. As long as the contradiction between what people intend to do and what they actually do is not apparent to organization members, as in the case of Jensen, there can be no improvement in innovation.

# NOTES

1. See, for example, Gerald Holton's foreword to *The Twentieth Century Sciences*, G. Holton (Ed.), New York: W. W. Norton, 1970. This section also draws on *Theories of Creativity*, M. A. Runco and R. S. Albert (Eds.), Newbury Park, CA: Sage, 1990. Several authors in the latter book describe the organizational context required to support creativity.
2. The "layered" model of culture is described by Edgar H. Schein in *Organizational Culture and Leadership*, San Francisco, CA: Jossey-Bass, 1985.
3. This is drawn from A. Sapienza's "Believing Is Seeing," in *Gaining Control of the Organizational Culture*, R. H. Kilmann, M. J. Saxton, R. Serpa and Assoc. (Eds.), San Francisco, CA: Jossey-Bass, 1985.
4. "How Culture Forms, Develops, and Changes, by E. Schein, in *Gaining Control of the Organizational Culture*, above, pp 27, 25.
5. The author is indebted to the personal correspondence of Ivan Jensen, MD, for his insights into organizational culture.
6. "Jensen A/S" is also a composite, meant to be reflective of many organizations.

# CREATIVITY: THE INFLUENCE OF STRUCTURE, SIZE, AND FORMAL SYSTEMS

This chapter continues the exploration of the third sphere of the Venn diagram—organizational characteristics. As stated in the prior chapter on culture, a "motivated" group of scientists is a necessary but not sufficient condition for creativity. In addition, both the human (i.e., cultural) and technical aspects of the R&D organization must support collaboration, intellectual challenge, candid and transparent communication, and willingness to take risks in order for novel science and technology to emerge.

Technical aspects of the R&D organization include structure, size, and such formal systems as recruitment, performance appraisal and reward, decision making and approval, and information systems. Because of their impact on creativity, these are the most important technical aspects for you to get right.

Before addressing the pragmatic questions of what structure, what size, and what formal systems are right, the chapter first discusses creativity: characteristics of creative scientists, keeping creative scientists creative, and improving organizational creativity. This section draws on the results of studies of the influence of social (i.e., organizational) factors on creativity.

# CREATIVITY

## Characteristics of Creative Scientists

What appear to be common to all creative people are the following characteristics: tolerance of ambiguity, curiosity, ability to perceive juxtapositions of seemingly disparate elements, self-confidence, and persistence.[1] Take Shelly as an example. In the beginning of her career she focused on a phenomenon that, in her words, had no "existential element—it was simply not an acceptable part of the discipline jargon." But she was able to tolerate the ambiguity of working outside the accepted conventions and also intensely curious to know the relationship between a cause and effect she had observed. She kept (in her words) "walking around the phenomenon." She even managed to convince one of her colleagues to share her curiosity and "walk around" the same phenomenon. When he did, the two of them collaborated on the experiment that would lead to Shelly's first breakthrough discovery.

In addition to her curiosity about the phenomenon, Shelly was also able to perceive juxtapositions that others had not noticed. She said about herself:

> I like to turn things upside down to see if they are symmetrical. Symmetry and asymmetry of models and theories are important to me. I think about what would be the consequences scientifically if the opposite of what was predicted were true.

Shelly's predisposition to "turn things upside down" echoes remarks made some years ago by Gerald Holton, an academic physicist and keen observer of science and scientists. He found that creative scientists were able to provide insight into a phenomenon "in a way that amounts to a special perception."[2] He went on to describe "sensitivity to previously unperceived formal asymmetries or to incongruities of a predominantly aesthetic kind" as common to creative scientists.[3]

Finally, consider how self-confident and persistent was Shelly. When she described her work in the small company, she commented:

> I don't remember any decisions one way or the other. The truth is, I just went on working. . . . As long as our salaries were being paid, as long as I had all the technicians I needed and the right equipment, I just kept on with the experiments.

If you are explicitly seeking creative individuals for your R&D organization, you want these personal characteristics as well as scientific and technical competence.

## Keeping Creative Scientists Creative

The very characteristics that make people creative—curiosity, drive, self-confidence, persistence—also make them difficult. Remember that Geoff described people on his staff like Shelly as those who, when they came into his office, "were going to be blunt—quite outspoken about what I had or had not done—and they were going to be demanding." Another experienced manager of R&D found that creative scientists tended to be "logical, critical, opinionated, clannish, and do not suffer fools gladly."[4]

Dealing effectively with creative individuals requires that you redefine your boundaries of what is acceptable. As Stefan noted in Chapter 3:

> I have scientists working for me who are very eccentric and yet very brilliant. When I am asked where I draw the line when they cause trouble, I say that I draw the line very far away. I try to keep these eccentric scientists from getting into trouble in the first place. But I understand what they're like and I understand that, if I don't have people like that, I will have a very mediocre institution.

More specific advice for keeping creative scientists creative comes from research in the field of creativity. Investigators have found, for example, remarkably consistent responses to the question of what inhibits creativity.[5] Creative people do their work because it is inherently interesting, enjoyable, satisfying. As a consequence, they do *not* respond to such extrinsic "motivators" as management pressure, project evaluations, or competition for rewards. Studies of scientists at the Center for Creative Leadership revealed that organizational factors were considered to be much more important than personal factors in inhibiting creativity. Prominent among the latter inhibiting factors were:

- constrained choice
- overemphasis on tangible rewards
- evaluation
- competition
- perceived apathy towards the project
- unclear goals
- insufficient resources

- overemphasis on the status quo
- time pressures.

Another investigator noted that an important organizational factor improving creativity was a culture that fostered wide sharing of information and communication among people with complementary skills.[6] This same researcher also stated that the discovery phase of creative work in organizations appears, to outside observers (such as top management), to be "slow, risky, and full of intermediate failure" (p. 156). Thus, managers of R&D must be prepared to buffer such creative work from the "powerful process-avoiding and process-terminating forces brought into play by uncertainty, fear of failure, intolerance of ambiguity, and pressures for quick and certain results" (p. 157).

## Improving Organizational Creativity

In addition to the above-mentioned research on creative individuals, there is persuasive evidence that the creativity of R&D can be improved.

One of the characteristics of creative individuals—variously defined as perceiving juxtapositions, as an ability to combine disparate elements, as sensitivity to asymmetries and incongruities—is associated with the use of particular *cognitive structures*. The latter are simply mental constructs or rules by which we process stimuli like sense data, thoughts, and images.

Cognitive scientists categorize cognitive structures into two types: rigid or fluid. Rigid structures are "tightly inter-constrained, so that one part [of the knowledge base] strongly predicts another."[7] Fluid structures, on the other hand, result in more creative thinking because they permit the knowledge base to be "turned upside down" (in Shelly's terms) and searched for what Holton described as "previously unperceived formal asymmetries" and "incongruities."

What is important for you as manager to understand is that people will use either rigid or fluid cognitive structures *under certain circumstances.* The same people who solve problems in a creative and flexible way (i.e., utilizing fluid cognitive structures) under certain conditions will solve them in a stereotyped and uncreative way (i.e., utilizing rigid cognitive structures) under other conditions.[8]

It should not be surprising to you that the organizational conditions associated with the use of fluid cognitive structures include ambiguity, collaboration, intellectual challenge, candid and transparent communication, and willingness to take risks. In R&D, the necessary organizational ambiguity can be achieved by ensuring, for example, that leadership of a working group is not determined by seniority or other formal mechanism but rather emerges according to expertise. It can also be achieved by ensuring that people do not perceive themselves to be in a superior–subordinate relationship but rather in a relationship of peers (this will be discussed in more detail below).

These organizational conditions were also found to be characteristic of high-performing companies able to adapt to new technologies.[9] An "organic" structure was the term given to the design of these companies. Characteristics of the organic structure, in addition to challenge and ambiguity, included informality, complexity, broad delegation of responsibility, and a lateral (horizontal) pattern of relationship and communication.

These findings are tremendously exciting, because they mean that the R&D organization can be designed in a way that stimulates creative thinking. In short: Creative thinking requires use of fluid cognitive structures, so that people are able to perceive juxtapositions (asymmetries or incongruities). Use of fluid cognitive structures is enhanced by the organic design. As the next sections will address more specifically, the creativity of R&D can be improved by the right organization structure and size, and the right formal systems (by, in other words, the right technical aspects).

## ORGANIZATION STRUCTURE AND SIZE

When we use the word "structure" we often picture an organization chart, with boxes neatly arranged in some logical order. However, as used here, the word has a more fundamental meaning. Organization structure is the pattern by which people relate to each other and communicate with each other. The organization chart, on the other hand, depicts the formally established lines of authority, which may be very different from how people actually relate and communicate.

There are two basic patterns or structures. One is vertical: superior to subordinate, pyramidal, or hierarchical relationship and communication. Another pattern is lateral: equal to equal (peer), network, or horizontal relationship and communication. Each pattern has been found to be more effective in certain situations.[10] Vertical structure is appropriate under stable operating conditions and in work processes for which rules and established procedures exist (these are algorithmic work processes). Lateral structure is appropriate under turbulent operating conditions (e.g., rapid change and high uncertainty) and in work processes for which few rules and established procedures exist (these are heuristic work processes).

In a lateral structure, people relate to each other as peers and, because of this, are more apt to collaborate (one quality of the creative R&D organization). Relating as peers, people are also more apt to communicate openly and informally (another quality of the creative R&D organization). Peer relationship and open, informal communication ensure that there will be fruitful debate and intellectual challenge (a third quality of the creative R&D organization).

Lateral structure also ensures the ambiguity on which the use of fluid cognitive structures depends. In a lateral structure, the person who leads each problem-solving effort is determined by who is the expert in the group. As problem topics change, problem-solving leadership changes. The answer to the question "who's in charge?" depends on the nature of the problem. For this reason, it is very difficult to draw an organization chart of a lateral structure, beyond listing those few individuals with formal authority.

Finally, lateral structure is a prerequisite of the organic R&D design, and lateral structure constrains size. That, in essence, is the relationship between creativity and the technical aspects of organization structure and size. Creativity requires lateral structure, and lateral structure constrains size. We can only relate as peers with those whom we know, and we can only know a limited number of people. We can only communicate openly and informally with a limited number of people. We can only engage in intellectual challenge with a limited number of people. Three of the conditions for a creative organization—collaboration, candid and transparent communication, and intellectual challenge—are incompatible with large (more than about 200 people) size. As a general rule, then, several small discovery units will be more innovative than one large unit.

When the work is heuristic—that is, it does not follow rules and established procedures, such as early research in novel areas—then the structure should be lateral (i.e., organic) and the size, therefore, small. When the work is algorithmic—that is, it *does* follow rules and established procedures, such as in late-stage development—then the structure should be vertical and the size can be much larger. As another general rule, a large development unit will be more productive than several small units.

But, when problems arise in a vertical design that require the use of fluid cognitive structures, then the problem-solving unit must be organic (lateral structure, small size). Small groups of people on task forces, or small project teams from appropriately vertical functions, must relate to and communicate with each other as peers, collaborating and challenging each other's ideas. Such groups must be informal, responsibility must be broadly delegated, and the pattern of relating and communicating must be lateral. These issues are discussed again under project management, Chapter 8.

## Management Implications

Because the vertical structure is so common, modeled as it is on the parent–child relationship, it is often the easier structure to design and manage. Work is divided by department, responsibility is clearly ordered, and there is a visible "top" and "bottom" to the organization. However, vertical structure is more effective only under stable operating conditions and in algorithmic work processes.

When conditions change (for example, turbulence increases), or when problems arise that require the use of fluid cognitive structures, then "more of the same" will actually degrade organizational performance. Unfortunately, this is usually the reaction of managers: to put in tighter controls and more explicit rules, and to put in place "über" bosses in the hope of arriving at a solution quickly.

The more effective approach is to identify smaller problem-solving group(s) and design a lateral/organic structure. To support creative thinking, you must rely on small size and organic structure. Assigning more people to a problem is likely to degrade performance. You must also encourage conditions that at first may feel completely wrong. In a lateral structure, ambiguity, lack of a designated leader, informality, and conflict are desirable. The organic structure appears to be a "messy" structure, but it improves organizational creativity.

## FORMAL SYSTEMS

The creativity of R&D is influenced by organization structure, size, and formal systems. For the R&D organization, the most important formal systems are recruitment, performance appraisal and reward, decision making and approval, and information systems. Like the culture, structure, and size of the organization, these formal systems must support collaboration, intellectual challenge, candid and transparent communication, and willingness to take risks. Each is discussed below.

### Recruitment Systems

Many recruitment systems are designed to find people who "fit" the organization. No matter what the rhetoric is about diversity, most recruitment policies and procedures are (unintentionally) designed to weed out personal style differences and intellectual differences from the majority. The consequences are conformity and uniformity, people who are unlikely to challenge the status quo, and lack of real creativity. As Stefan noted, not employing people who are eccentric in comparison to the norm results in a "very mediocre institution," despite what might be the glowing text of the annual report or other public materials.

To avoid conformity and mediocrity, you must actively

seek people who, at first, may make you uncomfortable because they are the "competent eccentrics." In other words, you must look for people who *don't* fit, who stand out in your mind as quite different from their colleagues.

Moreover, once the "competent eccentrics" have been recruited, you must support their eccentricities by encouraging them to voice *their* perceptions of "the world," and you must encourage others to listen to those perceptions, especially if they contradict what has been taken for granted. You are trying to improve organizational creativity by supporting and encouraging the use of fluid cognitive structures, and the eccentric is by definition more apt to perceive issues differently and thus to raise the creativity of the whole group.

You can also encourage "eccentric" thinking by bringing in visiting scholars, fellows, and other experts who are not in the mainstream but who may provoke your scientists to perceive juxtapositions by their very difference from accepted convention. Although not usually considered part of recruitment systems, policies for visiting scholars, etc., are certainly part of intelligent retention and training systems.

## Performance and Reward Systems

Like recruitment systems, many performance appraisal and reward systems unintentionally promote safe mediocrity. Consider the four qualities required for creativity. First, you must reward collaboration. This implies systems that take account of collective performance, such as group assessment of team activities, and reward collective performance as appropriate. Of course, group assessment is more complicated and time consuming than individual assessment. And group assessment assumes that you and your colleagues trust and respect one another's judgment of the people being reviewed, that you and your colleagues really value collaboration, and that the organization culture supports this value (Chapter 4).

Second, you must reward intellectual challenge. This means challenging your staff and encouraging them to challenge you—*really* challenge you, by disagreeing openly without fear of being publicly humiliated or privately rebuked. It also means being patient with the apparent confusion and delay in work activities that challenge may produce. When your scientists have argued and then come to some agreement about the problem, the solution will be much more creative than if you forced a solution. If you are a task-focused leader (Chapter 3), then rewarding intellectual challenge requires you to be *very* patient.

Third, you must reward candid and transparent communication. Again, you must model this type of communication and encourage it in your R&D organization. You must also be prepared for the fact that candid communication is not always good news—the bad is to be received as respectfully and thoughtfully as the good news. Many managers are surprised to discover that their scientists are unwilling to be open about problems or mistakes, preferring to send reassuring messages instead. Why? Because the manager has in effect punished candor by 1) reacting vigorously and negatively to the bad news, 2) immediately dismissing the sender until the problems are ironed out, or 3) rushing in to "micromanage" the issue, and so forth.

Finally, you must reward willingness to take risks. This implies that you are willing to reward people for what might appear to be poor results (not, of course, poor judgment) and you will *not* punish those who take a risk and fail. You might ensure that there is "free" seed money for experimental projects, money outside the traditional budget categories and not seen as coming from other committed allocations. You will also give wide visibility to those who have taken risks and succeeded. And you yourself should agree to take risks, even though you might fail.

## Decision Making and Approval Systems

Without intending to do so, many managers of R&D have designed, or accepted the design of, decision making and approval systems that are cumbersome, slow, and indicate lack of trust in the intelligence of the people involved. If you have hired intelligent people and encouraged candid and transparent communication, then very few *formal* decision-making and approval systems will be necessary. Certainly, the "big ticket" items or decisions will require a formal mechanism for approval, but it is surprising how many items or decisions do not, yet remain bogged down in these systems.

As Chapter 1 implied, R&D budgets should be developed in the context of overall organizational strategy and with the input and understanding of everyone in R&D. Then, the relevant units or departments should be given their allocation and be trusted to expend it wisely, even if you sometimes disagree with their decision (again, this is part of rewarding willingness to take risks and encouraging challenge). If there is a true spirit of collaboration in the organization, then appropriate "horse trading" can take place among units for spending that may exceed the budget of a specific unit. People should agree (and mean it) that all are working for the good of the R&D organization rather than the aggrandizement of their particular laboratory. You should have as one of your objectives that "turf" be defined as the whole of R&D, rather than one part of that organization.

Similarly, project decisions should be made by those closest to the issues. If communication is really candid and transparent in the organization, then the appropriate information will be communicated to management as a normal part of working together. If management input is needed, it will occur without decision rules.

## Information Systems[11]

Although you may not perceive them as such, information systems (of all the formal systems) can actually provide the most opportunities to enhance the four qualities of a creative R&D organization.

**Collaboration** can be supported by, among others, electronically linking scientists, no matter in what part of the organization they work; ensuring wide distribution (electronic or paper) of provocative material, including notes on work-in-progress within the organization; providing ease of (electronic) access to scientists outside the institution; and providing easy access to useful data banks.

**Intellectual challenge** can be supported by these same tactics, as well as by distributing information widely on a "want-to-know" rather than a "need-to-know" basis.

**Candid and transparent communication** can be supported by all the above, and by sending the good news as well as the bad news through the system with similar alacrity.

**Willingness to take risks** will follow if your information systems conform to these guidelines.

## SUMMARY

What can be said of individuals can also be said of organizations: Given the right fit of the human aspects of personal competencies and job demands, the technical aspects are secondary (this does not imply that they are unimportant). Thus, if the culture "works" (i.e., supports the qualities described in Chapter 4), then structure, size, and formal systems are secondary. If the culture does not "work," then no matter what you do in terms of structure, size, or formal systems you will not be wholly successful.

Too much time and energy are spent "tinkering" with structure, size, or formal systems. In this regard, less is always better. There are only a few rules of thumb to follow. If you want to improve organizational creativity, then the structure should be lateral and the size small. If operating conditions are stable and the work is algorithmic, then vertical structure is appropriate. If the work is appropriately conducted in a vertical structure, but a problem arises requiring the use of fluid cognitive structures, then you must design a small, lateral, organic unit within the vertical one. This is, in essence, what the matrix accomplishes (Chapter 8). If the work is heuristic, then you must design a lateral, organic structure and keep the organization small.

With regard to formal systems, the rule of thumb is likewise simple. Design them with the four qualities for creativity first and foremost, and you will get them "right."

## NOTES

1. See, for example, David M. Harrington's "The Ecology of Human Creativity: A Psychological Perspective," in *Theories of Creativity*, M. A. Runco and R. S. Albert (Eds.), Newbury Park, CA: Sage, 1990.
2. Gerald Holton, *Thematic Origins of Scientific Thought*, Cambridge, MA: Harvard University Press, 1973, p. 354.
3. Gerald Holton, *The Scientific Imagination*, Cambridge, England: Cambridge University Press, 1978, p. 281.
4. J. D. Fitzgerald, "Reflections on Some Problems in the Management of Drug Discovery," in F. Gross (Ed.), *Decision Making in Drug Research*, New York: Raven Press, 1983, p. 209.

5. This material draws on the work of Teresa M. Amabile, "Within You, Without You: The Social Psychology of Creativity, and Beyond," in *Theories of Creativity*, op. cit.

6. This material draws on the work of David M. Harrington, "The Ecology of Human Creativity," in *Theories of Creativity*, op. cit.

7. D. E. Rumelhart, P. Smolensky, J. L. McClelland, and G. E. Hinton, "Schemata and Sequential Thought Processes in PDP Models," in J. L. McClelland and D. E. Rumelhart, et al., (Eds.), *Parallel Distributed Processing*, Cambridge, MA: MIT Press, 1986, vol. 2, p. 37.

8. H. M. Schroder, M. Driver, and S. Streufert, *Human Information Processing*, New York: Holt, Rinehart & Winston, 1967.

9. T. Burns and G. M. Stalker, *The Management of Innovation*, London, England: Tavistock Press, 1966.

10. See, for example, Donald Gerwin's "Relationships Between Structure and Technology," in P. C. Nystrom and W. Starbuck (Eds.), *Handbook of Organizational Design*, Oxford, England: Oxford University Press, 1981.

11. This section draws on "Surviving as a Niche Player in the Pharmaceutical Industry," by S. Jorgensen, I. Jensen, and M. Edwards, *Drug Development Research 274*, 1993.

# C H A P T E R   S I X

# COMMUNICATING EFFECTIVELY

It should be so simple. You speak to another person, or write a memorandum, or send E-mail, and you expect that person to understand and act accordingly. After all, you have *communicated*.

But have you? Communication, which comes from the Latin *communicare*, to share or impart, is a complicated process and there are many ways in which something can go wrong. To help you communicate more effectively, this chapter explores three aspects of communication: 1) the process, 2) the message, and 3) the medium by which the message is transmitted. Examples of problems and of solutions are included.

## THE PROCESS OF COMMUNICATION

Let us assume that you want to communicate to your staff that there will be a hot water shutdown on Sunday from midnight to 4 AM because of routine maintenance. This task consists of six steps[1] (see Fig. 1).

- You, the *sender,* first *think* about the audience to whom the message will be sent and the information you want to impart.
- You *encode* the information by putting your thoughts into the communicable form of words, phrases, numbers, etc.
- You *transmit* the encoded message via some medium (airwaves, if you speak directly; paper or electronic media, otherwise) to the scientists and technicians who will be affected.
- The *receivers,* the people to whom you sent the message, must *perceive* it. They must hear or read the message.
- They must *decode* your message by translating it into their thoughts.
- Finally, they must *understand* the message as you intended.

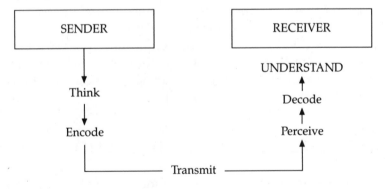

**Figure 1.** The communication process.

## Problems in the Process

To illustrate how complicated the process of communication really is, some of the problems that could arise at each of the six steps are reviewed below.

**Thinking.** You did not think carefully about your intended audience, nor did you realize the extent of the information that you needed to impart. Not only will the hot water be off for 4 hours, but also the heating units in a small-animal room. There are backup units on a generator, but maintenance personnel need at least 24 hours' notice for a non-emergency switch of heating power to the generator during weekdays. They require 72 hours' notice for a switch over the weekend, to avoid unnecessary overtime. You forgot about this advance notice when you sent the message on Friday afternoon.

**Encoding.** You sit at your PC and type out the following memo:

> TO       All Personnel in Building C
> FROM     Pat, Director of R&D
> DATE     Friday noon
> re:      Heating System Maintenance
>
> During routine maintenance of the heating system this weekend, there will be no hot water in the building for 4 hours on Sunday evening. Please contact the maintenance supervisor if this will present any difficulty.

In your haste to send the message, you left out the actual times of the shutdown.

**Transmitting.** You send the above memo via E-mail to all people in building C. However, your network software does not tell you that one node, the chemistry laboratory on the second floor, is offline. Their system crashed in a local power failure earlier that morning.

**Perceiving.** All people in building C, with the exception of those in the chemistry laboratory, have your message in their incoming mail file. Several scientists, however, neglect to check their computer for mail that afternoon.

**Decoding.** Some of the people who do check their E-mail read your message and wonder exactly what time the system will be down. A few decode "evening" as from 6 PM to 10 PM on Sunday and decide there *will not be* a problem. Others decode it as sometime after midnight and decide there *will be* a problem.

**Understanding.** The technicians responsible for the small-animal room read the message and immediately worry about the switch to generator-powered heating. They ask the head of the laboratory about the shutdown, but she is one of the scientists who has not checked her messages. By the time she reads it, they are all worried that you have forgotten the advance notice required. Or has the system been changed so that notice is no longer needed? If the system will be off between 6 PM and 10 PM, then the room may cool down too much. But, if the system will be off between midnight and 4 AM, they might not even need to switch to alternative power. Should they ask you or the maintenance supervisor?

Do not assume that most of the difficulties in the above example occurred because you were forgetful or that you used an electronic medium. Consider this scenario.[2] You are at your weekly staff meeting with 12 of your direct reports.

You announce: "We're expecting a few visitors from the corporate board on Tuesday, to see the prototype facility. Please make sure your people are prepared for them. . . . " While you are speaking, there are several "breakdowns" in communication.

**Distorted Perceptions.** Two of your staff are not paying attention. What they think they heard you say was something about the regulatory authorities. They begin to wonder what has gone wrong to bring in the regulators.

The director of the prototype facility hears your statement, but he takes it a step further. He envisions that the corporate visitors will be so impressed that they will insist the capabilities be expanded, and he begins to plan what equipment they might purchase. He ceases to hear the rest of your statement about the visit.

**Distrusted Source.** One of your direct reports does not believe that you, until comparatively recently an academic (as opposed to industrial) scientist, can understand the implications of a visit from the corporate board. She assumes that the board is concerned about company finances, of which you must be ignorant, and that these representatives are hunting for areas in which to make cuts. She begins to plan how to make her own area a "sacred cow" in terms of budget cuts and ceases to hear the rest of your statement about the visit.

**Distortions From the Past.** The assistant to the director of the prototype facility had a painful experience at his last place of employment. Board members came to visit his facility and, the next week, the entire group was laid off. He begins to panic, assuming the same thing will happen here, and starts mentally reviewing his curriculum vitae.

**Defensive Behavior.** One of your staff has been feeling very undervalued since completion of the state-of-the-art prototype facility. When she hears your announcement, she believes that the visit is yet another insult to her own production engineers. She interrupts and begins to argue with you about the budget for her department.

**Lack of Congruence.** When she interrupts, you ask her to hold off until you finish with the details of the corporate visit. You assume she does not care about the prototype technology, because she appears so argumentative. As a result, you are fairly brusque in asking her to wait. She assumes that you *really* undervalue her department and begins to think about updating her curriculum vitae.

Actually, the visitors from the board are three new members who worked at a corporation on the West Coast that used the same prototype technology. You know that they are very interested, and only interested, in one piece of equipment that your facility employs. But out of 12 staff members around your table, you have *communicated* this only to six.

## More Problems

In addition to the above, communication problems arise in every R&D organization because of *language barriers*. Language barriers between disciplines and functions can result in problems in the encoding/decoding stages of communication that preclude mutual understanding.

Each discipline in the R&D organization represents a group of people that shares a common meaning for their language, a meaning likely to be different from that shared by people trained in another discipline. For example, the word, "system," when used by a biologist (with implications for deviation-amplifying feedback), may be interpreted as "mechanism" by an engineer (with no feedback problems at all). What is "straightforward" for the physicist (conceptually) may be impossible for the biochemist (technically).

Even though people may be using the same words, they denote entirely different meanings to the different disciplines. When the biologist encodes "system," the engineer decodes "mechanism," and so forth. In communication theory terms, what occurs then is *erroneous translation*. That is why multidisciplinary communication is so difficult to "get right." People may talk to each other, but they do not communicate.

One scientist described his experience of communication between chemist and biologist in this way:

Chemists are people who have a high level of expectation that tomorrow will be like today. But you can only take up biology if you have a great tolerance for ambiguity. So, when chemist and biologist first meet, collaboration is very difficult and it can take 2 to 3 years of intense collaboration to produce mutual trust.

There are differences in language, differences in temperament, differences in perspectives, and differences in what chemists and biologists *do* with the same information. A number is "7.6" to a chemist, but to a biologist it is "7.6 ± 0.5," and that makes a *hell* of a lot of difference!

The chemist has to learn that high variability does not mean low significance. It takes a lot of mutual learning by the chemist and biologist who are trying to collaborate.

At a large research facility employing laser physicists, engineers, and physicians (among other disciplines), the director stated that, during interviews with new scientists, they are literally asked: "Do you speak physics or biology?" He noted that he spent much of his time dealing with language barriers:

> To manage a multidisciplinary group like this, you have to identify the language barriers and get people to admit they exist. I do a lot of "interpreting" for my scientists.

Communication problems also arise because there are language barriers between functions (e.g., research, development, engineering, manufacturing, sales, etc.). These barriers result from the fact that each function consists of people who specialize in certain activities and are therefore, by experience and training, differentiated from people in other functions.[3] Like different disciplines, different organizational functions represent groups of people who share the same meaning for their language.

Language barriers between functions are sometimes even more subtle than language barriers between scientific disciplines, because the terminology appears to be straightforward. People in research, for instance, may share a very different meaning of *time* from people in sales. A duration that is "soon" to a researcher may be protracted to a salesperson. And people in development may share a very different meaning of customer *needs* from people in marketing. What is an important innovation to a marketer may be unimportant to a development scientist, and vice versa.

Whenever people train or work together, whether in lengthy doctoral programs or by dint of experience in the field, they develop a shared meaning for their language that may not be shared by others with different training and experience. So, the *encoding, decoding, and understanding* steps in the communication process may be fraught with difficulty.

## Solution: Ensuring Feedback

To communicate effectively, you must understand how and why problems in communication arise. Then, you must ensure that *feedback* occurs throughout the communication process. (Remember: The person giving feedback to you becomes a "sender" and you become a "receiver.")

Consider the feedback that might be appropriate for each of the three earlier examples—the water shutoff, the board visitors, and language barriers.

**Feedback: The Water Shutoff.** *Thinking.* The first feedback loop in the communication process should always be to yourself. Before you encode a message, ensure that you have thought carefully about the intended audience and the information you want to convey. In this example, you might have 1) remembered to put in the exact time of the shutoff and 2) anticipated the problem for the small-animal room technicians.

*Encoding.* The next feedback loop should also be to yourself, by reviewing what you have encoded and comparing it with what you intended to say. In the case of written and electronic communication, you should ask someone to review and comment on the text before it is sent. If you had omitted the hours of the water shutoff, perhaps another person's query would prompt you to insert the time.

*Transmitting.* After a message is transmitted, you should seek feedback by strategically placed checks to ascertain that distribution actually took place. In this example, you should upgrade your network software to provide error messages if any node is offline. In the case of a written memorandum, telephone calls along the distribution route are advisable.

*Perceiving.* There is little you can do to ensure that all your staff read their E-mail or written memoranda, other than ensuring that you are selective in how much information is distributed in these ways. Information overload is one cause of problems at this stage.

*Decoding.* If you had neglected to put in the times of the shutoff, you would discover this omission when you asked key staff if they had any difficulty with the upcoming maintenance.

*Understanding.* Direct solicitation of feedback from your staff should also clarify the misunderstandings about the small-animal facility.

**Feedback: The Board Visitors.** Sorting out difficulties in communication while you are speaking requires an appreciation for the process and for the breakdowns that can occur, as well as sensitivity to nuances of expression (voice, facial) and other body language. On the basis of these cues, you might solicit feedback in the following ways.

*Distorted perceptions.* At your meeting, it was probably clear to you that two of your staff were not paying close attention. They may have been talking to each other, or catching up on their mail, or reviewing their calendar. To ensure that they understand your message, ask them if they have any special concerns about the visit. That would give them an opening to say: "What went wrong that the regulators are coming in?" And you could clarify the intended message.

Although it is impossible to anticipate that the head of the prototype facility will devise an elaborate plan for expansion after you mention "visit from corporate," a direct question might uncover the distortion: "Can you have this piece of equipment ready for a demonstration?" In his own mind, he was thinking about purchasing equipment, not demonstrating it, so you have provided an opportunity for clarification.

*Distrusted source.* In the example, you were the distrusted source because of your apparent unfamiliarity with industry. Assuming this is not your first meeting with the staff, then you have probably noted either an eagerness on the part of this scientist to bring you "up to speed" or cynicism when you describe your vision for the group. A useful direct question to her at the meeting might be: "Do you have suggestions for us in planning for this visit?" Let her elaborate on how she views the visit, and you can clarify the actual purpose.

*Distortions from the past.* As with distorted perceptions, you may not be able to anticipate how people perceive your message based on their own past experience. But if you seek feedback, then either you will discover at the meeting that this assistant is concerned about the visit (and you can reassure him), or the head of the facility will solicit his feedback and she can reassure him. At some point, distortions from the past will surface, if feedback is truly encouraged in the organization.

*Defensive behavior.* Your staff member who has been feeling undervalued gives an obvious clue that something is wrong when she interrupts to argue about the budget. You can clarify her misunderstanding of the purpose of the visit during your meeting, but you may need to confront her about the larger issue (discussed in Chapter 7).

*Lack of congruence.* If you respond to the tone of this staff member instead of to her implied message, you will escalate the miscommunication. There are two examples of lack of congruence in the example. First, she appears argumentative about the budget, but she is really worried that her facility is valued less than the prototype facility. Second, you appear to be dismissive about her group, but you are annoyed only at the interruption and apparent change of subject. You should inform her that you will meet about the budget, but this discussion is to inform everyone about the board interest in the prototype equipment.

**Feedback: Language Barriers.** If you have different functions and different disciplines within R&D, you have the potential for the communication problem of *erroneous translation* (e.g., the biologist encoding "system" and the engineer decoding "mechanism"). Many of these language barriers will disappear over time, as people work together and develop shared meaning as the result of shared experience. But you must ensure that people from different disciplines and functions also give and receive feedback and, as the director mentioned earlier, you must "interpret" between disciplines and functions as often as necessary.

For example, if you were at the meeting between biologist and engineer, you might ask the engineer what concerns she might have about the system under discussion, providing an opportunity for the biologist to explain about deviation-amplifying feedback. Similarly, when researchers and sales people, developers and marketers communicate, you should take the lead in asking simple questions about time, needs, cost–benefit ratio, and so forth. Do not assume, unless they have spent considerable time working together, that people from different disciplines understand what the others mean by these terms.

Ensuring feedback is a straightforward solution to many problems in communication. Asking direct questions, even at the risk of sounding foolish, provides the opportunity for clarification. In this way the receiver will understand the message as the sender intended.

In addition to understanding the problems that can arise and ensuring feedback throughout the communication process, effective communication also requires that you have an appreciation for the *messages* that are communicated. In the next section, a story about the acquisition of a small company provides an illustration of how, as messages become more complex and ambiguous, the opportunities for problems in communication can increase. As you read the following discussion among three scientists, be alert for occasions when there might be a *difference* between what these scientists say and what they might mean, and consider the implications of what they *do* say.


## THE MESSAGE THAT IS COMMUNICATED: AN ILLUSTRATION[4]

"Critical Care" is a multinational health care supply company with a growing business in hand-held blood chemistry and blood gas monitors for inpatient and outpatient use. The company's philosophy has been to grow by acquisition. Thus, when it became clear that biosensors represented the next frontier of technology for these devices, management began a systematic search for a startup company that might fit their core competencies.

Founded in the mid-1980s, "Gene-Chip" was one of the biosensor startups that had their origin in an academic institution. Between 1986 and 1989, the company raised almost $30 million in venture capital; it also entered a joint venture ("Pro-gene") with a chemical company whose management was interested in diversifying into medical devices. After the formation of the joint venture, a licensing scout from Critical Care decided that this startup was worth watching. Shortly thereafter, Critical Care worked out an agreement to acquire Gene-Chip.

In 1991, the founder of Gene-Chip, Jonathan Albright, and two managers from the central research division of Critical Care, Warren Farrell and Howard Bond, met to discuss how the two organizations might work together. Warren was then vice president of blood chemistry and blood gas R&D, and Howard was his director of clinical research. Their first subject was organization structure:

*Warren:*

At Critical Care, we look at the hospital and outpatient environment in terms of human anatomy, in particular major organ systems, and then organize along these lines. In each area we have preclinical and clinical directors.

What we call a "project" is the developmental phase of device production. What we call a "program" is the discovery phase. There's a director of each department, and the preclinical director coordinates all the programs. Currently, there are 10 research programs in the blood chemistry and blood gas area.

As soon as one proposed device stands out, top managers meet to decide if the device should move from program to project status. Then we have a project manager to oversee the next stage of engineering and clinical activities.

*Howard:*

In Critical Care's R&D organization, I think it is discovery that holds the most possibility for scientists to have rewarding and satisfying experiences. Once we get to projects, so much is developmental and structured.

*Warren:*

I think Critical Care's structure is a real advantage, because it breaks up the large mass of our central R&D into smaller components. The project managers report to the major organ area directors in typical matrix fashion. On each project team is a representative from the planning function, who reports to the director of project management.

*Jonathan*:

We have an entirely different approach to structure at Gene-Chip. First, we have a very independent, open attitude. All our laboratories are open. I've noticed that Critical Care's new facilities are small rooms, divided up. That promotes territoriality. We opened up Gene-Chip's space, with no territoriality. In fact, we don't have walls around the laboratory—you walk right up through the center of the laboratory instead of around a corridor.

Second, Gene-Chip is a young and very energetic company. We don't have corporate staff. Senior people with line responsibility report directly to the president. What we try to do is build a series of teams that looks at one basic problem. We give the scientists the opportunity to discover, but we also build critical mass around them so that whatever comes out can be moved forward rapidly.

*Warren*:

Well, I think that biosensors is clearly the next era for Critical Care and the entire medical device industry. Products will come from the marriage of biology and electronics, and that's where Gene-Chip fits.

*Jonathan*:

My goal is to bring Gene-Chip's new technology into Critical Care, to work with your resources and bring technology forward, to bring your biology groups new electronics principles. Critical Care has traditionally been a development company—you license products, develop them, and bring them to market. I think you're

**111**

entering a very interesting phase in the corporate life cycle, and the critical task will be to build a real research capacity.

I believe that Gene-Chip provides a very formidable research capability, and I think this acquisition will propel Critical Care into the next generation of technology and improve its position in developing advanced technology products.

*Howard:*

We have to be careful and find ways in which there is good complementation between Gene-Chip and Critical Care. We have to let our people in Critical Care do complementary and innovative work in the discovery process as well. The worst possible scenario would be for Gene-Chip to do the basic research and our group of scientists to be more and more developmental.

*Jonathan:*

But I think the medical device industry in general is an industry based on traditional engineering, and a major portion of Critical Care's work consists of careful testing and preparation of the documents required by the FDA [U.S. Food and Drug Administration, which oversees medical devices]—librarianship type of activity. Of course, it has to be done with tremendous care and in a particular manner. The major factor is getting to clinical trials, getting over the regulatory hurdles. I believe Critical Care will help Gene-Chip by teaching us the aspects of bringing devices to the market.

*Warren:*

The scientists who are affected most adversely by Critical Care's licensing, and that was the origin of this acquisition, are the biologists. They will be competing directly. For the engineers, it doesn't matter where the device comes from.

However, I think the competition will be positive. I think we are all aware we are in a competitive business. And that competitive approach carries over to your work, whether you're dealing with another company that has a device like yours, a licensing agent, or this acquisition. I think our biologists are always saying: "What can we do to overcome this new challenge?" From Gene-Chip, for example.

*Jonathan:*

I think the marriage of Gene-Chip and Critical Care will play itself out like all marriages: rocky. Territorial disputes will be the first major ones. Whose responsibility is what? And there will have to be some give and take in the management of money. But the principal assets of these two companies really fit. Critical Care's major market is in medical devices, but you had not built any electronics capability in-house. And we at Gene-Chip have not yet brought any device to clinical trials.

*Howard:*

I think there are fabulous scientists at Gene-Chip. My only concern is will they fit in at Critical Care, culturally? That's complex. I think they will help Critical

Care's culture evolve. In the end they will fit in, but it will be a different culture.

*Jonathan*:

I agree it will be a different culture. Even though you are acquiring Gene-Chip as a company, it brings an enormous quantity of new technology. It's *got to* bring Critical Care a different research culture as well.

## Analysis—Messages Sent, Messages Received

When Warren and Howard described the structure of Critical Care, part of their message—intended or not, and whether they were aware of it or not—was the impressive size of their research activity ("10 programs in this area"; the major organ structure breaks up "the large mass of the organization"). The cue to this implied message is Jonathan's defensive response about Gene-Chip: "We have an entirely different approach." Jonathan is also critical of the new physical facility at Critical Care, because it "promotes territoriality," and he contrasts Critical Care's R&D to Gene-Chip on other dimensions as well: age, energy, and bureaucracy ("it's a young and energetic company"; "no corporate staff").

Warren appears to be aware of a possible problem, because he tries to bring the three scientists together in his statement about biosensors as "the next era . . . and that's where Gene-Chip fits." Certainly they can all agree about that?

Not quite, because Jonathan's response begins to illuminate how he *really* views the acquisition. Jonathan believes that Gene-Chip is in a powerful position, because it contains the wanted and necessary new technology. He is very demeaning of Critical Care, describing it as "traditionally a development company," and he is not impressed with their research capability (essentially asking can they build a "real research facility"?).

Howard is worried. He warns them to be cautious, because the "worst possible scenario," in which Gene-Chip does the research and Critical Care the development, is in fact being described by Jonathan.

But Jonathan does not back down. He now couches his criticism of Critical Care in terms of the entire device industry, which is based on a "traditional" technology. Critical Care is, in Jonathan's terms, useful primarily for its careful "librarianship" and expertise in clinical trials.

Again Warren tries to find ways to reach some agreement among them, at the same time warning Jonathan that Gene-Chip will represent to the Critical Care biologists a "new challenge" to be "overcome."

Jonathan does not respond directly to this warning. He acknowledges there will be a "rocky" start to their working together and that "territorial disputes" will arise. But he may be implying that the territoriality will be on the side of Critical Care, because earlier he was adamant that Gene-Chip has no "territoriality."

Howard then voices an understandable concern about the cultural fit between his organization, Critical Care, and Gene-Chip, especially now that he has heard Jonathan. But Jonathan has the last word. His message is that Gene-Chip, with its "enormous quantity of new technology" will be the one driving not only new product discovery but also cultural change.

If you witnessed this meeting (or saw it on a videotape), you would find additional clues about messages sent and messages received. You could observe the "body language" of Warren and Howard from Critical Care and Jonathan from Gene-Chip and draw some inferences from that as well as their verbal language. Consider the following scenario.

Jonathan had just completed an hour's formal presentation on Gene-Chip in the large and well-appointed board room at Critical Care. When they started their discussion, the Critical Care managers, Warren and Howard, were comfortably leaning back in their chairs while Jonathan sat forward. Warren was at the head of the table leading the discussion, but Jonathan soon took over leadership by raising his voice somewhat and speaking more quickly and emphatically than Warren.

When Jonathan described Critical Care as "traditionally a development company," Warren and Howard looked at each other with alarm. Howard sat up and began to fidget with his pencil, then leaned forward and urged Jonathan to "be careful." Soon Warren was sitting forward, with Howard, and Jonathan began to sit back. When the meeting concluded, it was Jonathan who was sitting back and smiling at Warren and Howard, assured that they were in agreement with the importance and role of Gene-Chip in the evolution of Critical Care.

The solution to a communication problem of differences between what is said and what is meant, as well as the implications of what is said, is to ensure feedback. As discussed earlier, the same techniques—asking questions and clarifying what is intended—should be used.

In at least one real situation of the acquisition of a small advanced technology startup by a large firm, no feedback was sought. The president of the startup, like Jonathan of Gene-Chip, was confident that he was in the more powerful position and would rise to the top of the large company's management structure. But the acquiring company's management was very concerned over the apparent role reversal and put one of their managers in charge of the startup and brought the startup's president into company headquarters in a position with little influence. Many of the startup company's scientists left, because they had come into the company on the basis of the president's expertise. The former president was dissatisfied with his weak position, and left to start another advanced technology firm. For the large corporation, the acquisition essentially represented a $300 million mistake—a mistake that might have been avoided if real communication had taken place among the people who should have worked together.

The final aspect of communication to be explored is the *medium* by which the message is transmitted.

## THE MEDIUM BY WHICH THE MESSAGE IS COMMUNICATED

When we think about communication in organizations, we usually focus on the information to be processed. Communications theorists propose that there is a direct relationship between the *uncertainty* of the task and the *amount* of information that must be processed to accomplish it.[5] One important objective of organizational communication is to reduce task uncertainty by gathering, distributing, and sharing the appropriate amount of task-related information.

More recently, communications theorists have proposed that not only the uncertainty but also the equivocality or ambiguity of the task influence organizational communication. When uncertainty is high, more information must be sought; but when equivocality is high, it is not clear what kinds of information are needed, what questions should be asked, or what sources of data would help to reduce the ambiguity. To reduce the level of equivocality to the point at which the group can move forward and complete the task, members must exchange their perspectives and arrive at a shared agreement about the issues at hand.

In analyzing communication under conditions of high equivocality, communication researchers have found that certain media are more helpful in ensuring mutual understanding. Media that facilitate understanding of ambiguous messages are defined as *rich media,* because they allow immediate feedback, use natural language, and provide multiple cues about meaning.[6] Obviously, the richest medium is face-to-face communication, followed by telephone conversation and interactive electronic message systems.

If you think about the examples used earlier in this chapter, the one concerning the water shutoff would not be characterized by high ambiguity. If you left out the time of the shutoff and forgot about the advance notice to maintenance, you unwittingly raised the uncertainty of the task of dealing with the shutoff but not the equivocality. It is quite clear what information is needed (the time of the shutoff), what questions should be asked (what is the impact on the small-animal facility?) and what sources of data would help (you, and the maintenance staff).

The message about the corporate visit to the prototype facility, however, was ambiguous, as evidenced by the problems that arose during the meeting. Had that message been conveyed by a memorandum to all staff, however, the communication problems might have worsened.

*Lean media,* such as written or electronically distributed memoranda to the entire group, are essentially one-way means of transmitting messages. They are useful for straightforward and routine messages. But when the message is capable of more than one interpretation, as the board visit that was interpreted in several different ways, they should not be used. In the terms of communication theory, when equivocality is high, lean media cannot capture complexity and do not provide opportunities to give and receive feedback.

Another example of the need to match message to medium is provided by the acquisition of the biosensor company, Gene-Chip, by Critical Care. Imagine if Critical Care sent out, by distribution to all staff, the announcement of the acquisition. The scientists would be very worried about their role in discovery. Would they in fact work only on development? Should they begin to look for another job? Would they be required to move to another location? And so on.

## SUMMARY

When something is wrong in organizations, one cause is often described as "communication problems." There may in fact be communication problems in R&D such as those described above—with the process, the message, and the medium by which the message is transmitted. If so, then the explication of the issues and illustrations of feedback should help you address them and communicate effectively.

But there may be other factors that result in these problems: backdoor communication (circumventing channels), civil communication (no one challenges established procedures or traditional "wisdom"), gossip, secrecy, and backbiting. If any one of these "communication problems" occurs in your organization, then the root cause is likely the organizational culture (Chapter 4), not the process, message, or medium of communication. However, learning to confront effectively, as discussed in the next chapter, will be helpful in addressing the culture as well as improving the effectiveness of communication in your organization.

## NOTES

1. This model is based on that of Shannon and Weaver, 1949, and is discussed in *Organization Behavior* by Gregory Moorhead and Ricky W. Griffin, Boston, MA: Houghton-Mifflin, 1994.

2. See *Organizational Behavior and the Practice of Management*, by D. R. Hampton, C. E. Summer, and R. A. Webber, Glenview, IL: Scott, Foresman, 1978.
3. The phenomenon of organizational differentiation (addressed again in the following chapter) was described initially by P. Lawrence and J. Lorsch, *Organization and Environment*, Cambridge, MA: Harvard University Press, 1967.
4. This story is a composite and is not meant to resemble particular people or particular organizations but many people and many organizations.
5. See, for example, Jay Galbraith's "Organization Design: An Information Processing View," *Interfaces*, May 1974.
6. R. Lengel and R. Daft, "The Selection of Communication Media as an Executive Skill," *The Academy of Management Executive 2*, 225–232, 1988.

# C H A P T E R  S E V E N
# DEALING WITH CONFLICT

There is no organization without conflict. But not every disagreement is real conflict. As discussed throughout Chapters 4 and 5, challenge and candor are hallmarks of a creative R&D organization—and challenge and candor will inevitably produce debate and disagreement.

The real conflict that is the subject of this chapter is a disagreement that literally gets in the way of work. Real conflict produces indecision, uncertainty, anxiety, frustration, and often anger. (In contrast, the disagreement produced in a climate of intellectual challenge is full of enthusiasm and excitement.) In a situation of real conflict, much of people's energy is spent not on work but on trying to deal with their feelings. (Healthy disagreements result in more intense efforts, not less.) That is why you must deal with real conflict swiftly and effectively. To do so, you must first understand the source of the conflict. There is no use intervening unless you have some confidence that your solution addresses the problem. Without intelligent diagnosis, you run the risk of exacerbating an already troubled situation.

In addition to *power*—having it or not having it, or having it threatened—there are other sources of conflict. As stated in Chapter 1, this book makes the heroic assumption that everyone in R&D agrees with institutional strategy and its consequences; thus, power is not discussed as a source of conflict. Instead, the chapter describes four other potential sources of conflict in R&D (and every organization) and then discusses the most effective conflict-resolution method, confrontation. Brief vignettes of conflict-resolution, using characters from some of the prior stories, are provided to help you learn to confront effectively and, thus, deal with conflict effectively.

## POTENTIAL SOURCES OF CONFLICT

Like the word, "strategy," *conflict* is derived from battle terminology and means the striking together of opposing forces. Conflict implies difference, and the major sources of differences in any organization also represent the major potential sources of conflict.

It must be emphasized that these are *potential sources*— not every difference leads to conflict. This discussion focuses only on differences inevitably found in organizations that are also likely sources of (that is, they may lead to) conflict. You cannot eradicate sources of differences in R&D. But knowing where to look and what to look for will assist you in diagnosing and "treating" real conflict appropriately.

The inevitable sources of differences in the R&D organization are of two types: 1) individual and 2) organizational. Sources of individual differences include personality and diversity; sources of organizational differences include task interdependence and organizational differentiation. Each is described below.

# Individual Differences

**Personality.** Your and your colleagues' dominant work-related need (power, achievement, or affiliation) and associated leadership style (task- or relationship-focused) constitute the first source of differences and potential conflict. The reason, as implied in Chapter 3, is that the way you inspire others and direct them in a course of action, in decision-making, and in problem solving is in large measure determined by the above aspects of your personality (or the human aspects of your personal competencies). By the same token, how you communicate and how you confront conflict is also in large measure determined by these two aspects of your personality.

Differences in personality between individuals are a likely source of conflict because people may behave so differently when faced with the same issue (but they will perceive it and behave consistently with those human aspects of their personal competencies). If you have a high need for power coupled with a very task-focused style, you perceive the world and behave differently from a colleague with a high need for affiliation coupled with a very relationship-focused style. Thus, what you or a colleague may initially believe is stubbornness or willful disregard in another person may simply be a reflection of these differences. If they are not recognized for what they are, and if people believe that perception and behavior are emanating from willful disregard of the "truth," then conflict will result.

**Diversity.** In addition to being different by virtue of personality, people differ from each other by virtue of gender, race, ethnicity, age (what might be termed salient or tangible differences), as well as by education, background experiences, religion, political persuasion, and so forth. In an era of "political correctness" we are exhorted to value this diversity and we should, because the resulting differences in perspectives can improve organizational performance.

But diversity also brings with it belief systems about classes, of individuals that may slide over the "edge" into stereotyping. No human being is without these belief systems, which consist of propositions about how a particular class of individual should act or be. They are part of our human capacity to see patterns and draw inferences about relatedness.[1] Belief systems that become stereotypes, however, about how every woman, Asian, or .older scientist should behave are highly likely to produce conflict. The individual who holds a stereotype—for example, "older scientists have lost touch with the state-of-the-art"—is predisposed to act towards people in that class as if they *have* lost touch with their field. Moreover, people who hold stereotypes rarely perceive disconfirming evidence but "re-fence" their belief systems to exclude an anomalous individual. An older scientist who is in the forefront of the field may be put into another class, such as "MIT scientist," rather than "older scientist" by the person holding the stereotype, and so forth.

Diversity and stereotypes are not limited to gender, race, ethnicity, or age. People may hold stereotypes about academic versus industrial scientists, MBAs, Democrats, Mormons, salespeople, mid-Westerners, and so forth. Again, we cannot avoid belief systems about various classes, such as "the research of academic scientists is free of the constraints of commerce," but stereotyping all individuals in the class and then behaving in conformance with the stereotype is guaranteed to produce conflict.

## Organizational Differences

**Task Interdependence.** The nature of the work of research and development is a source of differences and conflict by virtue of the interdependence of the required tasks. Like personality and diversity, task interdependence cannot be eradicated, but it is a likely source of conflict at one time or another.

There are three types of task interdependence.[2] First, *sequential interdependence* implies that task A must be done before task B can be initiated, and task B must be completed before task C can start, and so forth. In the pharmaceutical industry, as an example, drug discovery (task A), preclinical development (task B), clinical trials (task C), production (task D), marketing (task E), and sales (task F) are sequentially interdependent tasks. A compound must be discovered (task A) before it can undergo preclinical development (task B), which must be completed before clinical trials can start (task C), and so on until the product is sold on the market (task F).

In sequentially interdependent tasks, conflict is likely to arise if one task is delayed, if the output from one task is not of the quality expected by people responsible for the following task, or if incomplete or insufficient information accompanies the product from one task to the next. In R&D organizations, the above-mentioned opportunities for conflict suggest the importance of ensuring efficient and effective project handoffs (this is addressed again in Chapter 8).

The second type, *pooled interdependence* implies that all the *input* tasks must be completed before the *output* tasks can begin. Pooled interdependence accompanies mediating technologies, technologies that link customers with the desired outputs, such as moving money from a bank to borrowers. Clearly, money must be accumulated via the input tasks of accumulating and investing it before it can be "output" as loans, etc. In the above example of pharmaceutical R&D, pooled interdependence occurs within the task of clinical trials. All the product and patient information from multicenter trial physicians must be gathered and processed by company personnel (input tasks) before the required regulatory documents can be submitted (output task).

In pooled interdependence, conflict is likely to arise if some of the inputs are received in nonstandard format, if too few inputs are received to produce the desired output, or if inconsistent processing of inputs results in inconsistent quality of output. Pooled interdependence requires the rigorous application of uniform standards to both inputs and outputs, and sufficient volume of inputs to warrant the output.

Finally, *reciprocal interdependence* implies that the output from one task (task X) is the input to another task (task Y), but the output from Y is the input to X as well. In pharmaceutical R&D, reciprocal interdependence occurs often during the discovery phase. For instance, the output from magnetic resonance imaging (MRI) (task X) is a molecular structure that is the input for chemical synthesis (task Y), and the output from chemical synthesis is a compound that will undergo MRI analysis. This iterative and reciprocal processing continues until the chemistry department is satisfied that the compound structure matches what was desired. (Of course, further testing in the following sequentially interdependent tasks may initiate these reciprocal tasks again and again, until scientists agree that the structure is "right.")

In reciprocally interdependent tasks, conflict can occur if either output is delayed, if either output is not of the quality required, or if incomplete or insufficient feedback accompanies either output. Note that the potential sources of conflict are the same as those in sequentially interdependent tasks, but the intensity of conflict is much higher (there is less "slack"). Of all types of task interdependence, reciprocal interdependence is most likely to produce conflict. In the R&D organization, reciprocally interdependent tasks should be physically close to one another, people involved in the tasks should reach consensus on the desired quality of outputs, and they should have a basic understanding of both tasks, to ensure that appropriate feedback will be given.

**Organizational Differentiation.** Research and development occur in what theorists describe as a complex organization that, because of its complexity, is *differentiated* in structure by discipline, specialty, skill, and function.[3] As described in both Chapter 1 and Chapter 6, each discipline, specialty, skill, and function represents a group of people who share common training and experience and a common language as well. However, each group is different along those lines from every other group. So, each different part of the R&D organization represents the final source of potential conflict.

Like personality differences, discipline and the other organizational differences result in a particular way of looking at the world and behaving in response to that perception. There are numerous amusing (and some not amusing) anecdotes about the differences between chemist and biologist, clinical physician and discovery PhD, academic researcher and industrial scientist, hardware engineer and software engineer, etc. Again, what appears to be intransigent or wrongheaded behavior on the part of a colleague may simply be a reflection of organizational differentiation. No one discipline suffices; all are required to do the work. But, organizational differentiation makes it harder to achieve teamwork and collaboration in R&D (this will be addressed again in Chapter 8).

# CONFLICT RESOLUTION

Confrontation has been found to be the most effective means of addressing the real conflict that may arise from the four sources of differences in the R&D organization, as well as conflict that arises over power. Of the array of possible conflict-resolution techniques, such as smoothing, compromise, forcing, or avoidance, confrontation is the only means that does not allow people's indecision, uncertainty, anxiety, or anger to linger and thereby detract from organizational performance.[4]

However, when most people read or hear the term confrontation, what is conjured up in their minds is an image of two red-faced individuals arguing heatedly. Certainly, one meaning of the verb confront is "to accuse," but the sense in which it is used in this chapter is based on its derivation from the old French term for sharing a common frontier. To be skilled in effective confrontation is to be skilled in finding the common frontier between you and another person. Such skill is essential for effective project management (Chapter 8) and for effective efforts to bring about organizational change (Chapter 9).

Confronting effectively is difficult, because it requires that you deal with emotion. Finding the common frontier between you and another person requires that you go beneath the surface, probing and exploring issues, to discover the common ground that you do share. And probing and exploring involve acknowledging your own and the other person's feelings as well as perceptions, emotions as well as ideas.

There are straightforward and common-sense guidelines for effective confrontation, which are described below. The following section provides examples of confrontation scenarios and dialogue, using characters from the prior stories, to help you confront effectively.

## Confrontation Guidelines

**Know Yourself.** Becoming skilled is effective confrontation begins with understanding your personality—work-related needs (Chapter 2) and leadership style (Chapter 3). In terms of confrontation, if your central tendency is to focus on the task, for example, you must be cautious not to neglect the feelings aroused in you and the person you confront. If your central tendency is to focus on relationships, you must be cautious not to avoid exploring areas that may be painful to the other person (and, therefore, painful to you as well).

**Have an Agenda.** Having an agenda reflects the fact that 1) you have thought about what may ensue during confrontation and 2) you have a plan based on your deliberation. The agenda can be

- written and distributed ahead of time,
- written and distributed at the meeting,
- reviewed orally at the meeting, or
- kept in your head.

There are reasons for each of the above tactics. Distributing a written agenda ahead of time conveys the message (cf. Chapter 6) that the other person should come prepared to the confrontation meeting. Distributing the agenda at the meeting, either in writing or orally, allows you to set the focus and sequence of the discussion, which may be helpful under certain circumstances. It is sometimes appropriate to take the other person off guard, if by doing so you believe you can reach your common frontier more quickly.

Keeping the agenda in your head is appropriate for the situation in which 1) you know the other person very well, 2) the issue you are confronting is minor, or 3) you believe you need to keep the person completely off guard to get at the root of the difficulty.

**Rehearse.** Effective confrontation requires that you think through the possible scenarios. In the best case, the person agrees with you immediately and you come to a resolution easily. In the most likely case, the person argues, and you have to counter a number of statements. In the worst case, the person "blows up," and you have to deal with strong emotions.

Thinking through confrontation in this way is an important learning tool. In the words of one prominent learning theorist, "mental rehearsal... increases proficiency."[5] To be skilled at effective confrontation, therefore, you must mentally rehearse.

**Choose an Appropriate Location.** As you plan your meeting, consider the messages conveyed by meeting in your office (you are in charge), meeting in the other person's office (you give them "home" advantage), or meeting in a neutral place. Before you call a meeting in your office or the other person's, in a boardroom, or in the cafeteria, reflect on the implications of the location and take them into consideration in your rehearsal.

If you choose your office, you are sending the message that you are in charge. If you choose the other person's office, you are in effect stating that you are both on equal footing. If you choose the boardroom, you imply that this is a very serious meeting. If you choose the cafeteria, you imply that this is not a very serious meeting.

## Confrontation Scenarios

The first two scenarios are based on the example in Chapter 6 of the meeting to discuss visitors from the corporate board. At that meeting, one of the communication problems, *distrusted source*, arose because of experience differences among the individuals (one source of diversity). In that example, the manager had come from academia to industry and appeared to be stereotyped as an "ivory tower" scientist by one of the staff.

**Differences in Experience (Diversity) as a Source of Conflict.** You ("Dr. A") have observed for some weeks that one staff member ("Dr. B") is not committed to your plans for the organization. She is cynical about your vision for the future, refuting a number of statements behind your back and arguing in meetings about your intended strategic direction. Worse, her cynicism is beginning to affect a number of the scientists who were originally enthusiastic. She has worked in industry since receiving her PhD and appears to have stereotypical views of academic scientists. After identifying this as the likely source of the conflict, you decide to call her into your office and confront her. You decide to keep the agenda in your head.

*Dr. A:*

Thanks for meeting with me this afternoon. I want to talk about some concerns I have about the way you and I are working together. I feel that you're not confident I can lead this organization.

*Dr. B:*

Why do you say that? I've never said you were unqualified. . . .

*Dr. A:*

You've never said to me that I was unqualified, but you're clearly less than enthusiastic about my plans for this group. I wonder if you're worried about me in particular or just academics who come into industry?

*Dr. B:*

I know you have the right degrees and scientific experience, but you don't have much understanding of corporate R&D. It's not like academia, where you can tackle a problem because it's interesting and not worry about the commercial consequences.

*Dr. A:*

Well, I think there have been changes in academia that you may not appreciate. I've always been interested in the application of my research to "real world" problems, and I had to seek corporate funding for much of my work. So, I have some understanding of the commercial implications of what we do.

But I also know you have enormous industry experience, and I would like to be able to use that expertise in building our capabilities. However, you appear unwilling to contribute in positive ways to our group discussions.

*Dr. B:*

I wasn't aware I was not contributing. . . .

*Dr. A:*

What I've observed, and this may have been unintentional on your part, is that you react very cynically to my ideas, putting them down without a good rationale, arguing with me, and not proposing alternatives. And what is now very worrisome is that other members of the staff, who were previously enthusiastic, are sounding much less committed to change.

I'm sure you don't intend to undermine my position, but perhaps you underestimate your influence with the group, based on your experience in the company. And it's that experience I want the whole group to be able to rely upon.

The manager would explore further the issue of academic experience versus corporate experience and the possibility of stereotyping, always returning to the "common frontier" of the best interests of the whole organization. Note that the manager made sure that the staff member faced the fact that her behavior was detrimental to the group, not just inappropriate to the manager. And the manager gave her the opportunity to acknowledge that she was unaware of her behavior's effects on others.

In the worst-case scenario, this person may be trying to sabotage the manager's efforts. In this case, the initial confrontation will serve to put the scientist on notice that this behavior will not be tolerated. The manager may have to set up another confrontation meeting, including a person from human relations and with a written or oral agenda, to help this person change or to find another position outside the group.

**Organizational Differentiation as a Source of Conflict.** In the second scenario another communication problem, *defensive behavior*, arose because of organizational differentiation: the production engineering versus prototype facility groups.

It was not until the meeting to discuss the corporate visitors that you ("Dr. A") realized how defensive this staff member ("Dr. C") was regarding his production engineering group. As you reflect on this over the next few days, you realize that the production engineering manager believes the prototype engineers are privileged because they are working with the state-of-the-art. The prototype engineers reinforce this perception because they appear quite unconcerned about pragmatic problems in manufacturing, key issues to the production engineering manager. You ask to see the production engineering group director in his office, and you keep the agenda in your head.

*Dr. A:*

I just wanted to tell you how much I appreciate your work with the production engineering group. As I think about the organization's future, this group will play a big part in achieving the new strategic vision of the corporation.

*Dr. C:*

It will. We have a superb group of engineers working at the cutting edge of computer-automated production. Three of them just presented a paper to the international society.

*Dr. A:*

Great! You must have recruited good people *and* managed the group so that they enjoy working here.

I also hope that your people and the prototype group will work closely together, because I believe the next breakthrough will come from their technologies.

*Dr. C:*

Well, we let them know if we're having a meeting to discuss our work, but they seem to be off in their own world most of the time. They just don't appreciate the practical problems of manufacturing.

*Dr. A:*

I'm sure they don't understand anywhere near the level of detail that you and your engineers do. But you and they can learn from each other. I really encourage you to see how you can be helpful to the director of that group. And I'll make sure she understands what contributions your group can make to the work they're doing as well.

The manager and the production engineering group director continue to explore how the two groups can work together for the common good of the technology as well as the company. In the process, the manager reinforces the director's value to the organization and agrees to meet with him and the director of the prototype facility, to encourage collaboration across the disciplines.

There have been two instances in prior stories in which conflict got in the way of work. One was the story in Chapter 2, when Geoff was promoted over Shelly. The other was the story in Chapter 3, when Lee moved a corridor of scientists. In each case, the conflict arose from differences in personality (work-related needs and leadership style).

**Differences in Work-Related Needs: Shelly and Geoff.** When Geoff was promoted, Shelly was hurt and angry. She spoke only if spoken to, and everyone in the laboratory was aware of how she felt. Consistent with his dominant need for affiliation, Geoff let this continue for nearly 3 months, avoiding the problem rather than facing Shelly with the painful truth that he would make the better manager. Consistent with her dominant need for achievement, Shelly had viewed the promotion as a deserved reward for her accomplishments, rather than representing a fundamental change in work expectations. She responded to the perceived oversight with hurt and anger.

In the following scenario, Geoff has asked Shelly during the second week after the promotion to meet with him in a neutral location, the conference room. He gives Shelly the agenda when they sit down ("rationale for promotion," "role of lead scientist," "importance of working together").

*Geoff:*

Look, I know you're upset, but we have to talk.

*Shelly:*

What do you mean? We have been talking. I told you the equipment we needed was delayed because of the strike. . . .

*Geoff:*

[Interrupting] You know what I mean. You've been very abrupt all week. It's clear that you're hurt about the promotion.

The promotion has nothing at all to do with the intrinsic worth of either one of us. You're the best scientist we have. It would have been foolish to pull you away from what you do best and jeopardize the potential breakthrough. I'm a competent scientist, but I really believe that I'll make a better manager.

Think about it. As the manager I can help you get all those supplies and equipment and technicians you need, and you can continue with the work you love to do. Don't be angry about this.

*Shelly*:

I'm not angry. . . .

*Geoff*:

You're acting that way and I'm very upset by it. You have been very curt during staff meetings, and everyone is aware that you're unhappy about the promotion.

I know it sounds trite, but we have to work together if the company is going to survive. That's why I wanted to talk to you.

During a lengthy and emotional meeting Shelly finally admits she was angry and hurt because she thought her accomplishments were not valued. Geoff continually reassures her and stresses her importance to the organization as a bench scientist. Back at work, Shelly slowly thaws. By the following week she and Geoff are talking animatedly about the experiment, as they did before the promotion, and staff are no longer concerned.

Note that Geoff has to face Shelly with her behavior and its consequences. He has to emphasize that he feels her anger and is upset by it, and he has to reassure her about her own importance. Emotions have to be recognized before Shelly and Geoff can move towards their common frontier— the survival of the company and the effective working of their group.

**Differences in Leadership Style: Lee and Dr. X.** At one point in the discussion between Lee and Stefan about their styles (Chapter 3), Lee described how she moved an entire corridor of physicists in order to create a place for another highly regarded scientist. She admitted that the director of the group that was moved was very angry about her decision.

Consistent with her task-focused leadership style, Lee neglected to take into account the full impact her decision would have on the people involved. She should have met with this director ("Dr. X") well before the move took place.

The scenario described below is an attempt to prevent Lee's task-focused style from precipitating a disagreement that will get in the way of the work of the institute. The meeting is set in Dr. X's office, before the move, and Lee has sent an agenda ahead of time ("laboratory space issues," "effective use of major equipment," "department contributions to overall strategy").

*Lee*:

Thanks for making the time to get together. I want to talk to you about the current location of your laboratory. I've been concerned that you are not as close as you might be to the equipment and colleagues with whom you work, so I've found another site in building A. It's much more convenient, and the space is better suited to the work you're doing.

*Dr. X*:

I hadn't found this location inconvenient. We have to set up appointments to use the other equipment, but that's worked out well. And I like this building.

*Lee*:

Well, I'm sure you're downplaying the inconvenience. Building A is much better, but I have another objective in suggesting this. You know Dr. Z? I know you agree that his work is important for our institute, as is yours. But right now there is no suitable location for his laboratory, except for this corridor.

It strikes me that the move would be a win–win situation for everyone. You gain more convenient space, Dr. Z gains a laboratory, and the institute gains two satisfied scientists.

*Dr. X:*

Ah—so you want to move Dr. Z here and that's why you're moving me out?

*Lee:*

[She is prepared for this.] Not quite. I really have been concerned with your location. In my vision for this institute your work, as well as Dr. Z's, is important. I want to do what I believe is best for the both of you. The advantages of the new location, for you, are quite obvious: equipment, colleagues, better physical space. And your old location is perfectly satisfactory for Dr. Z. You both gain. I want you both to be in the best possible sites, so I would like to arrange for this move in two months. What do you need me to do to help bring this about as smoothly as possible?

The physicist is disgruntled about moving, but Lee continues to reassure him that this move is beneficial to everyone. She lets him know that she wants the move to take place, but she is willing to listen to him. She keeps exploring to find the common frontier: better space for both scientists.

In this ideal scenario, Lee understands that she has to focus on the relationships between her and Dr. X, and between Dr. X and Dr. Z. After this meeting, she calls the directors together and discusses how they can plan the move so it will be least disruptive to everyone. Again, she stresses the gains for each and works hard at the meeting to ensure that Dr. X does not feel manipulated but can graciously concede that his laboratory will be better off in the other building. And she ensures that Dr. Z voices his gratitude to Dr. X for accepting the inconvenience the move will cause him.

## SUMMARY

There is no organization without conflict. Sources of differences in the R&D organization can also be sources of conflict. Not every difference will lead to conflict, but any difference can. Knowing where the sources of differences are in your organization will help you diagnose the problem correctly. And developing skills in confronting problems when they do arise will help you deal with conflict effectively.

## NOTES

1. There is a very interesting discussion of stereotyping and related issues by K. Deaux and M. Kite, "Thinking About Gender," in *Analyzing Gender*, B. Hess and M. Ferree (Eds.), Newbury Park, CA: Sage, 1987.
2. This material draws on J. Thompson's *Organizations in Action*, New York: McGraw-Hill, 1967. Successive organizational researchers have confirmed Thompson's insights.
3. Ibid.
4. The effectiveness of confrontation was noted by H. Thamhain and D. Wilemon, "Conflict Management in Project Life Cycles," *Sloan Management Review*, 31–50, 1975.
5. A. Bandura, *Social Learning Theory*, Englewood Cliffs, NJ: Prentice-Hall, 1977, p. 26.

# PROJECT MANAGEMENT

Managing a project (as distinct from an organization) is relatively new in management history and, like other management concepts, has its roots in military strategy. Project management is analogous to campaign or battle management, as opposed to "war management."

Project management was first used in the U.S. air and space industries. Traditional organization structures—lengthy hierarchy, vertical relating and communicating patterns, and clearly separated functions—worked well when the task was predictable and relatively little information was required by generalist workers to complete it. But when the task was complex and uncertain and required a multitude of specialists to interact in order to complete it, then an enormous amount of information had to be processed. Dividing this type of work into a horizontal grouping of related subtasks and assigning multidisciplinary teams to each subtask was found to be more effective. Eventually the subtasks became known as *projects* and the multidisciplinary teams as *project teams*. Today, project management is widely used in hospitals, large-scale construction, and the electronics, pharmaceutical, and information technology industries, among others.

Despite its wide applicability and the length of time it has been in use, managing projects successfully is not easy—it requires *genuine collaboration* among individuals with varied backgrounds and skills in the R&D organization.

## COLLABORATION

Collaboration, which means "to work together," is easy to define but hard to achieve. It implies literal contiguity (physical and/or interactive electronic) and that the end result will be represent more than the sum of the individual contributions.

Project management, the subject of this chapter, entails "formal collaboration." Informal collaboration arises because people *want* to work together. One scientist determines that she or he needs the input of another scientist, and so approaches that person. In these informal situations, the job of the manager is to remove any hindrances to collaboration. (This chapter also assumes that the norms of your organization, as discussed in Chapter 4, support such informal collaboration. If they do not, then you may want to skip this chapter and read the next chapter on bringing about organizational change.)

In contrast to informal collaboration, genuine project collaboration requires advance planning and very high interpersonal skills on the part of the project manager. Just putting people together in collaborative units like project teams does not mean they will collaborate. In fact, they generally will not. Achieving genuine collaboration requires an understanding of work motivation needs (Chapter 2) and leadership styles (Chapter 3), the capacity to design and maintain lateral structures (Chapter 5), and skills in communicating (Chapter 6) and confronting (Chapter 7) effectively.

But the ability to manage projects successfully is generalizable. That same ability will ensure effective collaboration between the research and the development functions, between R&D and other functions such as manufacturing, and between in-house R&D and external alliances. Moreover, the same ability will ensure effective collaboration between divisions as well as between organizations as a whole, such as two or more universities or institutes, or a merger of two companies.

As you might expect from the origins of project management, the project is really a microcosm of an organization. Multiple disciplines and/or functions are represented, and each contributes to a critical portion of the overall project. Work must be accomplished under resource (time and cost) constraints. Thus, the project leader is essentially a general manager, managing the project rather than a single function. Problems occur within projects that mirror those occurring within organizations as a whole. Fortunately, fewer people are involved in projects, so project management is often viewed as a testing ground for future general managers.

Consistent with the focus of the book, this chapter emphasizes behavioral, as opposed to technical, aspects of project management. There are numerous texts on the latter subject, and the field itself publishes an excellent "body of knowledge." This chapter discusses, first, the size, structure, and composition of the project team. Second, communication and leadership-style issues over the project life cycle are reviewed. Third, technology transfer, by which the "technology" (including an idea from exploratory research) is handed over to successive teams for further development, is explored. Finally, "matrix" structure is defined and described.

## THE PROJECT TEAM

Perhaps the best example of a formal collaborative unit is the project team. By definition, it consists of people from different disciplines (e.g., chemistry, engineering, epidemiology) and/or organizational functions (e.g., manufacturing, marketing, sales) who are chartered to achieve a specific goal ("conduct exploratory research in $X$," "build the $Y$ prototype," "test $Z$ to determine if development should continue," and so forth). Other formal collaborative units are task forces and committees (not discussed here) and the matrix (discussed later).

## Team Size

Contrary to what is practiced in many organizations, each project team should consist of three or four up to a maximum of seven or eight people. "Team" implies that the members are close knit; they are expected to interact frequently and over a fairly long duration (years, in the case of some exploratory research). A larger team is unwieldy for close interpersonal interaction and communication.

If the desired goal requires more disciplines or functions than seven or eight, then the group should be divided into subteams. Plenary meetings of the entire group can be held as needed, and the team leaders can meet among themselves to address issues common to all teams. Calling a group of 15 or 20 (or more) a "team" does an injustice to the concept and to the members who are expected to work as a unitary whole. The word, "team," after all, comes from the *small* group of draft animals used to pull a plow. (Too many were literally unworkable.)

## Team Structure

All collaborative units, from the smallest team to the largest matrix organization, are *lateral structures*. As discussed in Chapter 5, there are only two basic patterns (called structure) of relating and communicating in organizations: vertical, which involves superior to subordinate relating and communicating, and lateral (peer to peer). The so-called "diagonal slice," consisting of several reporting levels from multiple disciplines or functions, is also a lateral structure.

Lateral structure has been found to be the more effective pattern when operating conditions are turbulent and when there are few rules and established procedures, which usually characterizes the work at the start of a project. Lateral structure also promotes the intellectual challenge and ambiguity that is a condition of the use of fluid cognitive structures. Thus, lateral structure also increases team creativity.

In order to work together (i.e., collaborate), project team members must relate to each other as peers. From a scientific and technical perspective, the project manager or team leader is one among equals. The project manager is the formally designated liaison to the larger units from which members are drawn and is the "general manager" of the project. But exactly who directs team members in scientific and technical problem solving and decision making will depend on who has the expertise required. As the problems and decisions change, leadership in this sense must change as well.

Perhaps the most critical task of the project manager is to build the team. This includes keeping the size of the collaborative unit small enough so that people can interact and ensuring that their pattern of interaction is lateral (peer to peer). To support lateral structure at the start of the collaborative work, the project manager should:

1. disseminate all information to everyone;
2. *not* designate people for specific tasks ahead of time;
3. emphasize wide consultation (i.e., beyond members of the team);
4. call frequent, short meetings of the entire team; and
5. model and encourage wide-ranging discussion and close communication.

In a lateral structure people must also communicate laterally. But lateral communication in project teams can be extraordinarily difficult because of "language barriers." As described in Chapter 6, people from the same discipline will share a common meaning for words they use and will communicate effectively. When multiple disciplines are involved, as they invariably are in a project team, people may use the same words but they will mean different things to those in different disciplines. Consider this example from an experienced project manager in pharmaceutical R&D. He discovered the following.

When the chemist uses the word, "product," she means the new substance or compound that is shown to have some in vitro activity. When the formulation specialist uses the word, he means the substance that has been formulated into a capsule. When the physician uses the word, she means the packaged and labeled drug available for clinical trials. And when the marketing person uses the word, he means the approved and launched drug that will produce income. When early candidate management teams discuss the "product," there may be at least four different interpretations of the same word.

The same language problem occurs when multiple functions are involved. For example, people from research may use the word "soon" to mean months, but people from sales may understand the word to mean days. In communication terms, *erroneous translation* will invariably characterize multidisciplinary and multifunctional communication, unless the project manager ensures that feedback occurs within the team. Over time, of course, these language barriers should diminish, as people come to agree on shared meanings. But at the start of the project, the manager must interpret and translate as necessary, ask the apparently simple questions ("how long, in days, do you mean by 'soon'?"), and encourage team members to question each other freely, in order to clarify their meaning.

The lateral structure of teams must often coexist within a vertical structure (e.g., lateral research teams within vertically organized science departments). If this is the case, the project manager should try to buffer the lateral structure by providing separate meeting space (and separate work space, if at all possible). It is also helpful if separate reporting relationships can be instituted (e.g., the team is responsible collectively to all department heads from which the members are drawn, and the department heads are responsible collectively for the optimum functioning of the team).

## Team Composition

The technical composition of the project team—the requisite skill mix—must obviously be a function of the desired result. If successful exploratory research in a particular area requires expertise in molecular modeling, gene splicing,

147

chemical synthesis, and in vivo testing, then the technical composition of the research team must provide the appropriate disciplines and skills. If successful development of applications software requires expertise in Unix, C++, and multimedia, then the composition of the development team must include engineers proficient in these disciplines. From a technical perspective, the composition of the team is straightforward.

The human composition is also straightforward—it should, as far as possible, reflect a balance among work-related needs (Chapter 2). Ideally, a team should include three or four people with a dominant need for achievement, to drive the technical progress of the project, plus two or three people with a dominant need for affiliation, to hold the members together by dint of their attention to interpersonal relationships. The project manager, the formal administrative liaison, should have a dominant need for power or a dominant need for affiliation. If the project manager has a high need for affiliation, she or he must understand that people with a high need for affiliation are sometimes anxious about how well they are liked, and as a result, may inadvertently compromise organizational success by *not* making hard decisions affecting members of the project team. (See Chapter 2 on motivation and work-related needs.)

As a rule of thumb, the team leader should not be a person with such a high need for achievement that she or he ignores either the "big picture" or the internal, human, workings of the team. In many organizations there is a tradition to put the scientist who made the discovery in charge of the project team, without assessing that person's dominant work-related need. If the scientist is a "high achiever" like Shelly (Chapter 2), she is unlikely to appreciate the diplomacy, patience, and communication and confrontation skills required to develop and manage a multidisciplinary or multifunctional team and to deal with the competing demands of the discipline or functional heads. Better to appoint a scientist whose human aspects of these personal competencies fit the human aspects of the demands of the job of team leader (see the Venn diagram in Chapter 2).

## COMMUNICATION AND LEADERSHIP STYLES OVER THE LIFE CYCLE[1]

The familiar logistic curve illustrating the proportion of work completed over time (or the growth of populations over time, adoption of innovations over time, pattern of scientific citations over time, etc.) is useful for understanding some of the human issues that will occur over the project life cycle. There are four stages denoted on the logistic curve (see Figure 2):

1. formation or emergence stage
2. buildup stage (representing fastest growth over time)
3. main stage (when most of the work is accomplished), and
4. completion or termination stage.

In the formation and early buildup stages of the project, technical uncertainty will be highest. This is defined as the difference between the amount of information required to complete the work and the amount possessed by the project team at the start of the work.[2] One of the jobs of the project manager is to ensure candid and wide-ranging communication among members, in order to reduce technical uncertainty. Over time, technical uncertainty will decrease, and the amount of necessary information-processing activities will decrease as well.

*149*

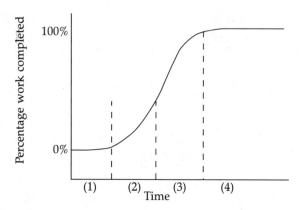

**Figure 2.** Project stages: 1) formation, 2) buildup, 3) main, 4) completion/termination.

Behavioral uncertainty is also highest in the formation and early buildup stages, because members have little information about reporting relationships within and outside the team, work norms, performance evaluation, and so on. Again, one of the jobs of the project manager is to reduce this behavioral uncertainty without compromising lateral structure (i.e., the peer relating and communicating must be maintained). Clarifying reporting relationships, norms, and performance requirements will again involve candid communication.

The formation and early buildup stages of the project are also likely to be characterized by high technical and behavioral *equivocality*. There may be multiple interpretations of, for example, the desired technical endpoint (this constitutes technical equivocality). When uncertainty is high, more information is needed. But when equivocality is high, members of the project team must exchange their perspectives and conflicting interpretations, to arrive at a shared agree-

*150*

ment on the *meaning* of the issues. To help accomplish this, the project manager must utilize a relationship-focused leadership style. As discussed in Chapter 3, a focus on relationships, to ensure candid and challenging discussion and reach shared agreement about meaning, will be more effective in reducing equivocality. If the project manager's style is task-focused, she or he must be careful not to impose structure on this particular communication process.

If both technical uncertainty and technical equivocality are high, equivocality should be reduced first. In the example of beginning research in a novel area, the project team must agree on the definition of scientific success before members can begin to reduce the technical uncertainty of how to achieve that success. From the perspective of the project manager, leadership style should be relationship-focused first and task-focused afterwards.

Like behavioral uncertainty, behavioral equivocality will also be high at the formation stage. Members of the team will undoubtedly have different interpretations of their team identity during the project. For instance, one member may become the project "cheerleader" (especially if the person has a high need for affiliation); another, the information coordinator; another, the linchpin to a specific external expertise. These roles cannot be specified in advance, but the project manager can help team members reduce this behavioral equivocality through a relationship-focused style of leadership (e.g., as these identity issues arise, the project manager brings members together for a candid discussion of their implications and consequences).

Interestingly, behavioral equivocality increases again at the completion or termination stage, because members of the team face the loss of their collaborative identity and the disruption of established interpersonal relationships. Again, a relationship-focused leadership style must be employed by the project manager, and she or he should spend the time needed to speak one-on-one with team members at this stage.

Over the course of the project life cycle, then, a relationship-focused style will be more effective in the formation stage, when equivocality (technical and/or behavioral) is high. During the buildup and main stages, a task-focused style will be more effective as uncertainty and equivocality are reduced. But during the completion or termination stage, a relationship-focused style will again be more effective, to deal with the increase in behavioral equivocality caused by breakup of the project team. Skill in communication as well as in matching leadership style to the requirements of the situation is especially vital to successful project management.

## MATCHING PROJECT MESSAGES TO COMMUNICATION MEDIA

The distinctions between *lean* and *rich* communication media (Chapter 6) are relevant to this discussion of communication during the project life cycle. To reduce the technical and behavioral equivocality characterizing the early stages, rich media (such as face-to-face communication) should be used. If the project manager does not involve members of the collaborative unit in face-to-face discussions at this time, their misunderstandings and conflicting interpretations will persist and may jeopardize the unit's performance. Moreover, the project manager must manage the communication process in such a way that disparate members are formed into a coherent and organic unit that characterizes an effective team. Candid and open communication, in other words, is an essential part of team-building.

When task and behavioral equivocality are reduced, leaner media (electronic and paper) can be used. However, the project manager should be sensitive to the "spikes" of equivocality that can occur over the course of the work. For example, the technical endpoint of the project may change midway through the effort, as the result of an unforeseen discovery or failure. To resolve the problems that will arise when the team must define a new endpoint, the project manager must utilize rich media for communication and a relationship-focused leadership style.

In the completion or termination stage, technical and behavioral uncertainty will be lowest, so lean media will be appropriate for task communication. But the rise in behavioral equivocality requires that the project manager use rich media to deal with the human (as opposed to technical) messages regarding members' next assignments. To sustain morale in the face of the impending dispersal of a cohesive unit, project communication *must* be face-to-face.[3]

# TECHNOLOGY TRANSFER

Complex research and development always involves multiple project life cycles in the idea-to-product process. For instance, in some companies involved in pharmaceutical R&D, discovery teams will identify a possible compound for further development. The compound will then be transferred to a preclinical research team that, if successful, transfers it to a clinical research team, and so on all the way to product sales. If there are $N$ phases or discrete steps to go from idea to product in your organization, there will be $N - 1$ transfers of technology across each of the *interfaces* between one project team and another.

If the research is in novel areas—if, in other words, the output from discovery will be a "breakthrough" innovation (as defined in your field)—the early transfers or project handoffs are most likely to be *rate-limiting steps* in the overall process. Why? The early transfers across the interface will be characterized by high equivocality. Because the innovation represents a "break" from the past, there will be little past knowledge and experience to guide the solution of problems that arise in the next stage following discovery, and the stage after that. Both the problems and their potential solutions will be open to multiple and conflicting interpretations by members of the two teams, and these conflicts must be resolved before further development can take place.

During these early handoffs, the most important aspects of the project to be transferred are in fact the knowledge and experience gained by the prior team. But when the transfer is characterized by high equivocality, then a special form of communicating that knowledge and experience across the interface is required for the handoff to be timely and effective. What is required is transactive (or two-way), interpersonal communication.[4]

Complicating this situation, many research facilities, especially discovery facilities, are often geographically distant from development facilities. The transactive, interpersonal communication required for technology transfer to be timely and effective will not occur unless it is carefully planned and managed. The effectiveness of the early transfers, and the overall speed of bringing the idea to the user, will be contingent on how well the knowledge and experience gained by the discovery team are communicated across the interface to the subsequent team.

Ideally, all members of these teams should be able to communicate face-to-face whenever necessary. But when organizational units are geographically distant, the project manager has three choices.[5]

First, the manager can plan to bring a few scientists from the development team to work with researchers and then communicate the knowledge and experience to their own team face-to-face when they return with the tangible or intangible innovation. In communication terms, these peo-

*154*

ple are called *receiver representatives* (the members of the research team are the *senders*).

Or, the manager can plan to bring a few scientists who once worked in development into the research team, to communicate face-to-face with researchers and present the viewpoint of development, to help solve the problems of the particular handoff. These people are called receiver *surrogates*. Surrogates would be sent, with the relevant innovation, to the development team, to communicate the suggested solutions face-to-face.

Third, the manager can bring a few scientists with expertise in development to work in a consulting capacity and communicate face-to-face with both the research and the development teams. These people are called receiver *integrators*. Like the surrogates, integrators would literally carry the innovation and communicate the knowledge and experience of the researchers to the development team face-to-face.

In making the choice among representatives, surrogates, or integrators, the project manager should consider the following. If the research and development teams are geographically close, then use of representatives may be most feasible. As geographic distance increases, rather than remove organizational members from their facility for a length of time, it may be better to use surrogates (if available), or integrators. If people from the same organization (surrogates) are available, they may be preferable to consultants (integrators). In either case, the manager should try to match the national culture of surrogates and integrators with the national culture of the development team. For example, if research takes place in England but development takes place in Germany, then experienced German nationals should be sought. Matching cultures in this way facilitates the communication that must accompany handoffs across large geographic distance and national cultures.

As an example of the *receiver* model, Takeda Chemical Industries, the largest Japanese pharmaceutical company, has a basic research facility in Tsukuba, several hundred kilometers from their development facility in Osaka.[6] When a discovery is made by the research scientists, development scientists are brought from Osaka to Tsukuba, to work side by side with researchers in preparation for the handoff. The development scientists then return with the compound, as well as the knowledge and experience gained (and transferred) by the research team, to the Osaka facility.

Timing the overlap of team members is also critical. There are two peaks of behavioral equivocality during the project life cycle: in the formation stage, and in the completion or termination stage. Because of this second peak of behavioral equivocality, representatives, surrogates, or integrators should be brought into the research team *during the main stage* of the research project. The timing of all face-to-face meetings between research and development teams should coincide with the main stage of the research life cycle. If face-to-face meetings are arranged for the completion stage, the handoff will be unnecessarily protracted. Researchers will be dealing not only with the high equivocality of problems associated with further development of the breakthrough innovation but also with the high equivocality aroused by the impending dissolution of their team.

## THE MATRIX

A matrix is defined as a *network of intersections*. In organizational terms, a matrix consists of the intersection of functions or disciplines (as vertical columns) with projects (as horizontal rows). Because each member of a project team comes from a functional department and is assigned to the project, she or he operates in a matrix. The person from, say, software engineering who is on the ABC Project Team (with marketing, manufacturing, and other functions) operates at the *intersection* of the software-engineering function and the ABC project. Each person in the team reports to two "bosses": the project manager, and the functional head. The software engineer is responsible to the project manager for achieving, with other members, the team charter (i.e., the project goal). At the same time, he or she is responsible to the head of the software-engineering function for the caliber of his or her technical contribution to that project.

When research and development entail a complex mix of people from different disciplines and functions who must collaborate, the collection of projects itself may be organized as a matrix. In such cases, the project manager is responsible to the head of project management for completion of the project on time and within budget, and to the functional heads for effective deployment of functional resources.

The matrix concept may, in fact, apply to many levels of the organization. The corporate level of Hoechst, A.G., the multinational German chemical company, is designed as a matrix. Each major business has a head, and each major function (such as research, development, engineering, manufacturing, etc.) has a head. At the corporate level, the head of "pharmaceutical research" (the intersection of that business and that function) reports to both the head of the pharmaceutical business and the head of the global research function.[7]

Within Hoechst's pharmaceutical business, each therapeutic area (e.g., cardiovascular, antiinfectives) is organized as a separate business unit, containing research, development, marketing, and engineering functions (among others). Within the therapeutic area organization, the head of cardiovascular research, for example, reports to both the head of pharmaceutical research (who, in turn, is "matrixed" to the corporate level, as above) and the head of the cardiovascular business unit. Within the research teams, members report to both the project manager and their respective discipline heads, and so on.

The matrix requires equal sharing of performance evaluation between, for example, the project management function (or equivalent) and the scientific and technical functions. Although the discipline heads are responsible for the technical caliber of team members, overall assessment must be based on the project outcome and the performance of the team *as a team*. Individual members receive two evaluations: for the project accomplishment, and for the caliber of their functional contribution. But teams must be assessed on the basis of project performance and rewarded on that basis as well. Collective rewards, tangible and intangible, are important. The project manager should ensure that evaluation, criticism, and praise are given collectively.

For obvious reasons, such a complex organization design as the matrix is not to be adopted lightly. It is, however, the structure of choice when information from the demand side of the business is as important as information from the technical side; when, in other words, the market environment and the technical environment are turbulent. If scientific or technological *and* customer requirements are changing rapidly, then neither a functional (technical) nor a product/customer (demand) structure will be effective. Under conditions of technical and demand turbulence, when information from both arenas is critical to organizational success, matrix structure is most effective.

What makes the matrix difficult to manage is the need to maintain a balance between technical and demand requirements. This network of intersections, from the project level to the corporate level, exists at the metaphoric point of inflection between scientific/technologic information on the one hand and customer information on the other. The matrix "sits" on a fulcrum; science and technology cannot drive the collaboration, nor can the demands of the customer. The solution must always be a joint solution.

As a result, the project manager is always caught in the middle. The project manager represents the customer, in the sense of understanding the potential use of the innovation, even in a discovery team and before any input from the traditional customer functions like marketing or clinical medicine. The project manager will always be in the cross-fire between the requirements of the potential user and the requirements of the scientific and technological disciplines that contributed to the innovation. These conflicts are never resolved to the complete satisfaction of the different functions, but they must be resolved to the complete satisfaction of the *project*. That is the fundamental and inherent paradox of the matrix.

For the above reason, if effective project management is highly dependent on communication skills, effective matrix management is highly dependent on confrontation skills. Because the project manager works at the intersection of the project and the disciplines, she or he will always be working to find the common frontier between the project and the disciplines. In the abstract, this frontier is the effective completion of the project and successful transfer of the innovation to the next team. In day-to-day work, however, the frontier will not be so easy to find.

Each discipline will perceive its contribution as critical to overall project success. This conflict, between project and discipline, endures for the life of the project. That is why the project manager must be able to bring the discipline or functional heads, again and again, to recognize and agree upon the common frontier. The project manager lacks the authority to force a resolution in favor of the project; he or she cannot compromise the project, nor can the project manager avoid the conflict. Although the project manager might try to smooth this conflict occasionally, the most effective resolution is through confrontation. Matrix management re-quires, as Jay Galbraith noted more than two decades ago, "complete commitment to joint problem solving and shared responsibility."[8] Achieving this commitment requires con-frontation.

## SUMMARY

Skills in managing intragroup dynamics (the project team) are eminently generalizable to managing intergroup dy-namics.

The successful project manager understands what "for-mal collaboration" means and the planning it requires to be effective. She or he knows how to keep the collaborative units small enough for people to interact closely and how to choose the members of these units on the basis of their technical competence *and* their work motivation needs, as far as possible. The successful project manager has the in-terpersonal skills to build a team, by ensuring peer relation-ships among the people who should collaborate and by dismantling any language barriers to their lateral commun-ication.

The project manager does not lay claim to expertise in solving all problems but is confident in the problem-solving expertise of legitimate experts, no matter what their orga-nizational title. This is one key to the success of general managers.

The successful project manager is able to keep the "big picture" in mind.

The successful project manager understands that manag-ing the beginning and ending stages of the project *well* is critical to overall performance. He or she is sensitive to the patterns of technical and behavioral uncertainty and equiv-ocality over the life cycle and is able to match leadership style, as well as the medium of communication, to the requirements of these situations. Finally, the successful project manager is capable of balancing competing pressures on the collaboration and can always discern the common ground that everyone shares (and help them to discern the common ground themselves). The person who has successfully managed projects should also be able to manage the collaboration between the research and the development functions, between R&D and other functions such as manufacturing, between in-house R&D and external alliances, between divisions, and between two organizations. The person who has successfully managed projects is an effective general manager.

# NOTES

1. Much of the material in this section is drawn from "Task and Human Messages Over the Project Life Cycle," D. Stork and A. Sapienza, *Project Management Journal 23*, 1992, 44–49.
2. This definition is based on Jay Galbraith's *Designing Complex Organizations*, Reading, MA: Addison-Wesley, 1973.
3. See "Phasing Out the Project," by H. Spirer and D. Hamburger, in *Project Management Handbook*, D. Cleland and W. King (Eds), New York: van Nostrand-Reinhold, 1988.
4. C. M. Avery and R. W. Smilor, "Research Consortia," in F. Williams and D. Gibson (Eds.), *Technology Transfer: A Communication Perspective*, Newbury Park, CA: Sage, 1990, pp. 93–108.
5. The recommendations are based on D. Leonard-Barton, "The Intraorganizational Environment," in *Technology Transfer*, op, cit., pp. 43–62.
6. A. Sapienza, "Takeda Chemical Industries," Harvard School of Public Health case study, 1989.
7. A. Sapienza, "Hoechst Pharmaceuticals: Making the Matrix Work," Harvard School of Public Health case study, 1987.
8. "Organization Design: An Information Processing View," by Jay Galbraith, in *Organizational Planning*, J. Lorsch and P. Lawrence (Eds.), Georgetown, OH: Irwin-Dorsey Ltd., 1972, p. 68.

# MANAGING CHANGE

## FIVE STATEMENTS ABOUT CHANGE

- No organization is perfect. Much of your time and energy as a manager will be spent trying to change the R&D organization in small as well as in fundamental ways.
- Because of the turbulence of the environment (see Chapter 1), the ideal R&D organization must be a flexible and learning organization, experimenting in behavior as well as in science.
- Achieving a flexible and learning R&D organization requires courage, focus, and persistence. It involves numerous painful processes, and it takes a long time. (Recent articles in the popular press have noted that managers can spend 2 years simply ensuring that peo-

ple in their organization *understand* the need for change, before that change can be brought about.[1])

- Because of environmental turbulence, today's solutions will become tomorrow's problems. Moving from a technology focus in R&D to a customer focus may be appropriate now, but the next science frontier may require a different focus. In some respects, your solutions sow the seeds of future problems. You will *always* have to manage organizational change.

- Because of environmental turbulence, there must be a paradigm shift in the way you manage. To manage change successfully, *you* must first change from relying on algorithms (i.e., standard operating procedures) to developing appropriate heuristics (i.e., general rules that require you to seek feedback as to their applicability).[2]

This paradigm shift in management is, in fact, reflected in this book. If you have read the chapters sequentially, or at least read most of them before reading this one, you will realize that there are few recipes for what to do (which may make the material disappointing and somewhat frustrating at first). This chapter, too, contains no recipes for managing change. Rather, two schools of thought regarding organizational change are reviewed and suggestions are given as to when and how each is effective. Then, an effective change effort is described in general terms. Finally, a story of people who have attempted to make fundamental changes in their organization, to achieve the ideal of flexibility and learning, is discussed. You should be able to derive your own heuristics for managing change from this material.

The emphasis in this chapter is on *fundamental* organizational change (to be defined later), although the heuristics can be applied to change processes of any scope.

# TWO MODELS OF ORGANIZATIONAL CHANGE

## Behavior Is a Function of Context

This first school of thought about organizational change is based on the assumption that people's behavior is a function of the external context in which it occurs. Therefore, to change behavior, you must change the physical surroundings, incentives, punishments, reporting relationships, etc.

Laws are based on the assumption that behavior change requires external context change. For example, laws concerning equal employment opportunity or workforce diversity have been enacted to change hiring practices by means of externally applied incentives or punishments (such as fines for noncompliance). They do not attempt to address any internally held stereotypes or prejudices that underlie an organization's restrictive, exclusionary hiring and promotion practices.

Another example of changing external context is changing the *formal structure* of the organization. "Reorganizing" is certainly a popular tactic undertaken to change behavior. Consider the earlier statement of having to change to a customer focus in R&D. In many organizations this is (presumably) accomplished by reorganizing R&D into end-customer units, along with changing the reporting, the information, and the reward systems. Usually, however, the reasons for a lack of customer-oriented behavior in the first place are not considered or addressed.

This school of thought—changing behavior in organizations requires a change in the external context in which behavior occurs—is founded on behaviorist psychology. A particular stimulus elicits a particular response, which can be reinforced by means of rewards and/or punishments.[3] In the above example of R&D, the stimulus of reorganizing is believed to elicit the response of customer-focused behavior, and this behavior is reinforced by changes in the reporting, information, and reward systems.

Is context change successful? Sometimes. People who have never worked with anyone of a different skin color but are required by legislation to move towards a more diverse workplace may discover that their initial stereotypes and prejudices disappear as they work together. On the other hand, there is ample evidence that, if laws are not actively enforced, people do not comply with them (speed limits are a good example).

Change in the external context by itself produces, at best, short-term changes in behavior. It may be appropriate in crisis situations, but genuine changes in how people think and work are not accomplished this way. In the above example of reorganizing R&D into customer units, genuine customer focus is unlikely to emerge. What will happen, instead, will be a veneer of customer-oriented behavior that widely misses the intent. Many quality-improvement efforts founder for the same reason: What led to the inappropriate behaviors in the first place was not considered or addressed.

## Behavior Is a Function of Attitude

The second and contrasting school of thought about organizational change is based on the assumption that people's behavior is a function of their internal attitudes. Therefore, to change behavior, you must change attitude.

Alcoholics Anonymous and other 12-step programs are based on the belief that attitudes towards drinking (or eating, gambling, etc.) must be changed in order to change behavior in a fundamental way. Primary care disease prevention efforts are based on the belief that a healthy lifestyle is brought about by changing people's attitudes towards health and wellness, and so on.

This school of thought—changing behavior requires a change in the attitude underlying behavior—is based on the so-called field psychology of Kurt Lewin and underlies the specialty of *organizational development*.[4] Lewin stated that an individual's attitude and, hence, behavior, is changed in four steps:

1. There must be a felt dissatisfaction with the status quo.
2. There must be an unfreezing of old behaviors (that is, disinvestment in old behaviors and receptivity to new attitudes).
3. There must be a conversion to the new attitudes (and new behaviors).
4. The new attitudes and ways of behaving must be internalized and institutionalized ("freezing").

There is a large body of evidence supporting Lewin's model as the more effective means of bringing about genuine and fundamental change and of achieving a flexible, learning organization.[5] However, the two schools of thought, although based on very different assumptions, are not mutually exclusive. There is an important place for behaviorist tactics to change external context in the second as well as the fourth steps in the above model of changing internal attitude. That is, to help unfreeze old behaviors, and then to support new ones, external context change can be invaluable.

The major distinctions of the models can be summarized as follows:

- The basic premise of the behaviorist model is that behavior is a function of external *context*; the attitude model assumes that behavior is a function of internal *attitude*.

- What prompts behavior change in the behaviorist model is *external* to the person (i.e., in the context); in the attitude model, it is *internal*.
- The rate of change is generally *faster* with the behaviorist model, *slower* with the attitude model.
- The personal involvement of the manager is *less* in the behaviorist model, *more* in the attitude model.
- In the behaviorist model, the duration of behavior change is a function of the duration of the changes in the external context. Behavior "reverts" if the context changes or is not enforced. In the attitude model, the duration of behavior change is a function of the depth of people's commitment to new ways of thinking, no matter how the external context changes.

How you might bring about organizational change using Lewin's attitude model is described generally in the next section. More specific examples are given in the story that follows.

# MANAGING ORGANIZATIONAL CHANGE

There is persuasive evidence that genuine and fundamental change in organizations is brought about more effectively by the four steps described in Lewin's attitude model, supported by changes in the external context. Fundamental change is any change in the *culture* of your organization (Chapter 4). For example, if the norms of your organization support a "technocentric" focus, then moving towards more customer-oriented behavior requires a fundamental change. If the norms of your organization support risk-aversion, then moving towards more risk-taking behavior requires a fundamental change. If the norms of your organization support limited and hierarchical communication, then moving towards candor, transparency, and lateral communication requires a fundamental change, and so on. What you as a manager might do to change these norms (i.e., the culture) is discussed below.

## Producing a Felt Need for Change

The first step in the change process, defined by Lewin as "felt dissatisfaction with the status quo," occurs readily under conditions of crisis. By then, however, you have usually run out of the time needed to bring about genuine, fundamental change. Thus, when you realize change is critical to the survival and success of the organization, your first task is to convince others of the need to change. This is a time-consuming effort, especially in large organizations, but fundamental change will not occur without the visceral appreciation—by at least a critical mass of people—that current behavior is not satisfactory or conducive to survival.

To bring about a felt need for change, you might design a two-part communication process. The first part could entail having articulate and persuasive speakers present to members of the organization "what is happening" in the environment, in the field of science, to competitors, etc. The purpose of these presentations is not to *tell* people that they must change but to describe vividly what is happening "out there" and allow them to draw the appropriate inferences. The more dramatic the evidence, the more likely people are to draw the inescapable conclusion: change is required.

Repeated emphasis of the external conditions, buttressed as much as possible by data about your own organization,

*169*

is crucial to bring about this first step. Framing it as information to be understood and then responded to by everyone in the organization also empowers (in a genuine sense) those who must be part of the solution.

The second part of the communication process could entail charging small groups of people to discuss the implications and consequences of change for the organization, openly and candidly. These small group discussions would begin as soon as possible after the initial sessions on "what is happening." By this time you would have discerned those colleagues who, like you, were convinced of the need for change. You might use them as discussion leaders. In any case, you would keep the composition of these small groups as heterogeneous as possible, using the so-called diagonal slice of the organization (across disciplines and functions, as well as up and down levels).

As manager, you must also model the desired new behaviors. If you were trying to change from "technocentric" to more customer focused, you would involve people from the customer functions in your small groups and really listen to them. If you were trying to change from hierarchical to lateral relationships and communication patterns, you would ensure that your small groups were run as lateral structures (review the material on managing project teams in Chapter 8). In all cases, the most important behavior for you and your discussion leaders to model is that of *learning*, by asking such probing questions as: "How did we get where we are?" "Why did this occur?" and so on. No learning can occur without feedback.

The objective of this step of managing change is to ensure that, as far as possible, everyone understands why change is necessary. The communication strategy described above should involve the whole organization, so your time frame will be dictated by the number of people who must hear the message. But your small-group discussions, with their appropriate modeling of new behaviors, would begin to generate solutions and to galvanize the critical mass required to move the entire organization in new directions.

## Unfreezing

Modeling new behaviors starts you on the second step, "unfreezing," which is undeniably the most painful step of the process. Each person must admit that "the old ways" of thinking and behaving are not appropriate. Externally, the environment is no longer predictable. Customers no longer accept whatever you produce. Politicians and legislators question the utility of discovery efforts and the amount of money spent on basic research. Communities scrutinize the safety of your R&D processes, equipment, and facilities, and so on. Internally, people may have become complacent. They may have accepted mediocrity without questioning their level of performance. There may be tacit agreement that some sloppiness is tolerable, and so on.

This second step of the change process requires great courage. Although it takes time, it is easier to generate an appreciation that external conditions necessitate change (i.e., to produce a felt need for change) than to give up personal behaviors that have been successful in the past, to admit that how you currently view the world may be mistaken, and to behave in radically different ways.

It is at this step that context change can be very useful. If you are trying to incorporate more customer focus in R&D, *and* a sufficient number of people in R&D now agree that such a change is required, *and* you have begun to identify why you lacked this focus in the past, then actual reorganization into customer groups should provide supportive context for the new behaviors. If you are trying to bring candor and transparency into your communications, and have the luxury of designing new facilities, then designing glass-walled and open laboratories will support such openness. Again, though, any change in external context will only support the internal attitude change; it will not produce it.

More specifically, achieving genuine customer focus might entail

- undergoing the pain of admitting your organization does not have such a focus;
- probing the causes of the problem (for example, the company was founded and succeeded initially because of technical expertise, resulting in the assumption that anything produced by R&D will automatically be acceptable to the customer);
- confronting "technocentric" behaviors whenever and wherever they occur (for example, behaviors that reflect the assumption that anything produced by R&D will automatically be acceptable to the customer); and
- consciously adopting new behaviors, even though initially they will feel uncomfortable and strange.

Similarly, achieving candid and transparent communication might entail

- undergoing the pain of admitting your organization is not open;
- probing for the causes of the lack of openness (for example, the way to get ahead in the organization is to compete individually; therefore, "hoarding" of information occurs);
- confronting old ways of communicating (e.g., impersonal memos, E-mail to distribution); and
- adopting uncomfortable and unfamiliar behaviors,

such as admitting openly that candor feels uncomfortable and unfamiliar.

## Conversion

This third step of organizational change is appropriately named, because attitude change involves the intellectual as well as emotional turning from one set of beliefs to another. Changing to more customer focus in R&D, for example, will require turning *from* intellectual and emotional adherence to "technocentrism" *to* intellectual and emotional adherence to genuine concern for customer needs. Likewise, changing to candid and transparent communication will require turning *from* intellectual and emotional adherence to secrecy *to* intellectual and emotional adherence to genuine openness.

During this step, the manager's understanding and support of the emotions of people undergoing conversion to new behaviors are crucial. If unsupported emotionally, people may not be able to sustain the change effort. At this step, especially, you need to be enthusiastic and encouraging, communicating in vivid terms and modeling the desired characteristics of the "new" organization.

When you do communicate, carefully choose the symbols and imagery you use, because they will become the new iconography of the organization. For instance, if people describe the "old" organization as a set of "towers" (or "silos," or other symbols of closed, vertical systems), use an ellipse enclosing departments when you illustrate the proposed lateral structure. If the old myths are couched in the language of battle, reflecting internal competition, start new myths by constant repetition of the language of collaboration. Listen carefully to yourself and your colleagues, and reflect on the implications of your symbolic language. Make your choices thoughtfully.

# Freezing

By this step, the manager should have a critical mass of people in the organization with a visceral understanding of the need for change (felt dissatisfaction), who are disinvesting in the old ways of thinking and behaving (unfreezing), and who are committing themselves intellectually and emotionally to new beliefs (conversion). The fourth step is internalization and institutionalization of the new ways of thinking and behaving. In short, the new ways must become habitual and consistent throughout the organization, until the next change effort is required.

To accomplish this institutionalization, changes in the external context can again be useful. If you have reorganized R&D into customer groups, you would ensure that your recruitment, performance appraisal and reward, decision-making and approval, and information systems (Chapter 5) supported the new norms. In addition, you would be scrupulous in modeling the new behaviors yourself and in confronting the slips and recidivism that would inevitably occur.

# Resistance to Change

There is wide agreement that organizational change *always* produces the syndrome of "resistance to change" (usually described as if it were a disease). Certainly, fundamental change is likely to result in changes in the established power centers. Hidden agendas and obstructionism are not uncommon reactions of people who find their power base shifting or eroding.

Ideally, if you succeed in producing a real appreciation of the need to change ("felt dissatisfaction with the status quo"), even people whose power is diminishing will agree that change is necessary and the alternative can be zero power for them if the organization fails. But if that first step is not effective, people will question why they must disrupt established practice, and they will try to convince you that you're tampering with something that does not need to be "fixed."

Some people may not agree that the world is changing and, therefore, believe the organization need not change. A few people have enormous capacity for denial, and nothing will shake them. In this case, you have several options. First, you (or an assistant) can spend intense one-on-one time with them to understand their reasoning and then respond in a way that may be persuasive. This is an appropriate tactic if the person is, for example, an upper manager whose commitment to the change effort is necessary. Or, you can tell them that they will have to conform with the new ways, no matter how they feel about it (this is the conflict-resolution method of *forcing*, and it must be accompanied by an explicit "or else"). Or, you can change their context by, for instance, assigning them to a very enthusiastic group that is wholeheartedly adopting new behaviors. You must be careful, of course, to ensure that one person's denial does not dampen the group's enthusiasm.

Some people may agree that change is necessary but hold fast to their power. As much as possible, you should try to ensure that both these people and the organization can "win" in the change effort. Otherwise, you may have to encourage them to seek work elsewhere.

## Commitment: Top Level, Bottom Level, or Both?

You may wonder if change will only occur if top management is committed, or if it will only occur if the "troops" are committed. In fact, both top and bottom levels must be committed. Your boss and your cleaning staff must be committed to change, and everyone in between!

The following story of a change effort in the R&D function of an Italian pharmaceutical company should give you more ideas and models (heuristics) for your own situation.

## PREPARING FOR A GLOBAL FUTURE[6]

The environment of the pharmaceutical industry in all industrialized nations presented a number of problematic issues and trends in the 1980s, including pressure from governments seeking to hold down medical cost inflation, changing demographics and epidemiology (resulting in a marked shift from acute to more chronic diseases), and the need to incorporate the technology of genetic engineering into the traditional medicinal chemistry research process.

Managers of "Bio-Farmaco," a large, family-owned Italian pharmaceutical company, were very uneasy about the ability of their organization to succeed in that environment. In 1986 they started a process to make fundamental changes in the organization. Aware themselves of the changed environment and the need for Italian pharmaceutical companies in general to move from a domestic to a global strategy, Bio-Farmaco management began by communicating these issues to all employees.

Over an 18-month period, the 7,000 or so employees became aware of the external changes, and scientists in R&D began to question management about the appropriate response. Once managers understood that the scientists were dissatisfied with the current state of affairs, the unfreezing process could begin. Interestingly, unfreezing was precipitated by shocking (to employees) statements from top management. For example, in all his communications to employees, the owner of Bio-Farmaco urged them to do something that most would consider very strange:

> You should abandon the thought that you have only to do what you are told by your supervisor. I want you to discuss problems actively, and exchange your opinions regardless of rank and division.

The owner's commitment to a new way of communicating was reinforced by the chairman of the company, who emphatically counseled employees to contradict their company creed:

> I don't want vague and questionable harmony in research and development. Good and fruitful debate is important. Don't hesitate to contradict our creed. Don't hesitate to take a risk!

As originally articulated in the 1800s, Bio-Farmaco's creed had a number of articles, including the importance of seniority and conservative behavior. The injunction to ignore this creed by both the chairman (overtly) and the owner (tacitly) was all the more powerful coming from top management and the owner of the company. To long-time employees, these statements had enormous shock value.

Within the R&D division, managers supported the unfreezing by modeling new behaviors, as well as by changing the context in several ways. One context change was to invite sales and marketing people to meetings formerly attended only by scientists, to discuss research findings and compounds for development. Another context change was to require the scientists to acknowledge their personal critiques of the compounds that were discussed. A third context change was to rotate people on project teams. Alessandro Domenico, senior director of R&D, explained:

*Alessandro*:

At first, scientists were reluctant to put their names on the evaluation forms used in these meetings with sales and marketing. But I want them to take that responsibility. They may be right or wrong, but at least they'll learn.

Moreover, I now try to have development decisions made by fresh people, because sometimes the scientists have been too influenced by their own past experience. So, I rotate some people within the project teams.

In the eyes of his colleagues, especially at the start of the change process, Alessandro was considered an anomalous manager as he modeled the new behaviors:

*Alessandro*:

My colleagues think I have done many unusual things in R&D, and they have told me that I look like a charismatic director, instead of a rational or scientific director. But what's important in discovery? Is it reason, or is it intuition?

Other context changes were made to the physical facility itself. The directors of the chemistry and biology laboratories renovated the offices so that they both shared a central reception area. As the director of chemistry said: "This way we're *sure* to speak with each other," effectively bridging the formerly separate disciplines in a way required for future research success. Similarly, a new building for the delivery system laboratories was being constructed in a style very different from the traditional facilities on Bio-Farmaco's campus. Giovani Bracca, the director, stated:

*Giovani*:

In the new building we have designed the laboratories to be open, with many people sharing office and laboratory space. In addition, people from several departments will have facilities on the same floor, to help make the organization more flexible.

Of course, more important than the facility is selecting the right scientists. We need to challenge established thinking, and we need people who will help us challenge it.

The most radical departure in architecture, and another example of context change, was the new basic research facility about 50 kilometers from headquarters. Unlike the conventional buildings on their main campus, Bio-Farmaco's building on this greenfield site consisted of glass-walled research laboratories and discussion areas surrounding a three-story marble atrium. The ground floor dining room looked out on a barbecue corner, where family parties were held in the summer. This architectural change in context was designed to support a radical departure in organization structure as well. Andrea Malatesta, manager of the facility, commented:

*Andrea*:

We will only have about 50 PhDs at any time, and we will focus on the underlying sciences. Bio-Farmaco's impetus to set up this basic research facility was our recognition that the Italian universities were not doing as much of this kind of research as we needed for our future survival.

Our group will have no organizing fields, like therapeutic areas [most applied pharmaceutical research is organized by disease or therapeutic area]. Instead, we encourage researchers to look outside the fields for new projects.

All scientists report to me. It is all bottom-up, no top-down. I believe young scientists should not be squashed by a top-down system, as has happened in this company.

The type of people I look for here have a special philosophy of research. I look for intuition, curiosity, and an ability to challenge.

Thus, in addition to top-down exhortations to contradict the company creed and challenge established procedures, to rotation of scientists, and to architectural change, managers were also looking for a different type of scientist to recruit. For these new people, challenge would (it was hoped) come more easily.

By 1990, Bio-Farmaco had reached the third step of their change process, conversion. One very important intervention at this step was the imagery repeated by Alessandro's assistant director, Maria Santa La Rocca. Maria spent much of her time with the R&D scientists, exhorting them in the following way:

*Maria*:

I tell scientists that they must become "pookas." These are mischievous spirits who can go through walls and fly freely beyond borders. Why? These scientists must overcome the very high, very thick walls, hurdles, and barriers set in the vertical structure of our organization.

Scientific creativity will be stimulated by person-to-person contact. We have to train our scientists to achieve lateral communication, and this is one way to encourage them.

My hope is that scientists will take on the *real* character of this spirit, who flaunts "rules" of society and who passes through rather than breaks down vertical barriers, and will catalyze our organization in all the ways needed for future success.

The pooka is a complex character. It is not simply a spirit but can be seen as the alter ego to the "civilized" or "cultured" individual. When Maria exhorted scientists to *become* pookas she was, in effect, exhorting them to become like that alter ego—nonconforming and creative, engaged in debate rather than harmonious consensus, and willing to undertake the risk of innovative and different research and development activities. She encouraged the scientists, in other words, to disrupt their normal order and to overcome organizational barriers by becoming organizational ghosts.

To summarize the change effort at Bio-Farmaco: Top managers began in 1986 with an intense process to educate employees about the volatile and competitive global environment of pharmaceutical companies, to help produce a felt need for change. In 1987, the owner and top management began publicly to encourage employees to challenge their superiors and to contradict the company creed, to help unfreeze their attitudes. In support of the unfreezing, a number of context changes were made. These included open physical space, rotation of scientists (to establish lateral relationships throughout R&D), and new management systems requiring signatures. By 1990, when the company was at the third step, conversion, Maria's imagery of the pooka was a powerful tool, helping people envision the new organization. The institutionalization of new behaviors (freezing) was supported both by the physical changes and by management system changes (new hiring and rotation procedures, new information systems, new organizational structures).

The result? The lead time for new pharmaceutical products is about 10 years, so Bio-Farmaco is coming to the end of that period. Already, however, the company has moved into the top 20 of the "world league" of the pharmaceutical industry because of increased sales outside Italy. They have funded several U.S. and other European academic centers conducting biotechnology research that have recently shown promise in the treatment of cancers (scientists are sent from Bio-Farmaco each year to these centers for training in the new technology). They have set up many successful joint ventures with U.S. and European companies, both to comarket products and to conduct applied research. By these standards, they are much better prepared for a global future than they would have been with no change effort.

In a smaller organization, such a fundamental change as undertaken by Bio-Farmaco might have been accomplished faster (in 2 or 3 years). But Bio-Farmaco's experience was· consistent with that of other effective change processes. It was time-consuming, required great courage on the part of managers to renounce established procedures, everyone suffered the pain of admitting to past mistakes, and there was inevitable backsliding. Bio-Farmaco's owner and managers persisted, and the results today reflect their determination.

## SUMMARY

As should be clear from this chapter, much of every organizational change effort consists of communication and, therefore, its success depends on your skills in effective communication (see Chapter 6). The entire first step, producing a felt need for change, is often no more and no less than communication of the external conditions prompting change, and of the internal issues that are problematic, given these conditions. Unfreezing consists primarily of communicating first to oneself and then to others that the old ways of thinking and behaving are no longer appropriate, and of probing to discern why and how those ways became problematic. And conversion can be helped or hindered by the imagery with which the vision of the new organization is communicated.

Successful organizational change also depends on your skills in effective confrontation (see Chapter 7). When people refuse to acknowledge the new external conditions, they must be confronted. When people avoid questioning why problems arose, they must be confronted. And when people display the old behaviors, they must be confronted.

As always, *knowing yourself* is important in managing change successfully. If you have a dominant need for power (see Chapter 2), you are likely to enjoy the challenge of aligning organizational behaviors with the requirements of the external environment and to do well in this endeavor. If you have a dominant need for affiliation, you are likely to enjoy the interpersonal involvement of the change agent and to do well in this role. Because successful change requires both activities, consider what complementary assistance you might need.

You will also have to adjust your leadership style (see Chapter 3) throughout the four steps. In the first and second steps, a task-focused leadership style will be more effective, because the issues are unambiguous—external conditions are changing, and internal behaviors are not appropriate. But in the third step, conversion, a relationship-focused style will be more effective. For some time during this step there will be different interpretations of the vision of the new organization, and a focus on relationships, to ensure wide and challenging discussion of these interpretations, will be required. In the fourth step, a task-focused style will again be more appropriate, because of the reduced ambiguity of the situation (the institutionalizing of the new ways of thinking and behaving).

There are no recipes for managing change, but there are useful guidelines. This chapter has reviewed a number of them; it is up to you experiment and to find more.

## NOTES

1. Brian Dumaine, "Times Are Good? Create A Crisis," *Fortune*, 28 June 1993.
2. See Stafford Beer's *The Brain of the Firm* (2nd ed.), New York: Wiley, 1981.
3. A. Bandura, *Social Learning Theory*, Englewood Cliffs, NJ: Prentice-Hall, 1977, .p 154.
4. Kurt Lewin, *Field Theory in Social Science*, New York: Harper & Row, 1951.
5. Michael Beer, *Organizational Change and Development: A Systems View*, Santa Monica, California: Goodyear Press, 1980.
6. This case study is a composite and not meant to reflect particular people and particular organizations but many people and many organizations.

# INDEX